KU-271-575

THE
Healthy Lawn
HANDBOOK

LANE
L.
WINWARD

LYONS & BURFORD,

PUBLISHERS

Copyright © 1992 by Lane L. Winward

ALL RIGHTS RESERVED. No part of this book may be reproduced in any manner without the express written consent of the publisher, except in the case of brief excerpts in critical reviews and articles. All inquiries should be addressed to: Lyons & Burford, 31 West 21 Street, New York, NY 10010.

Printed in the United States of America

10 9 8 7 6 5 4 3 2 1

LIBRARY OF CONGRESS CATALOGING
IN PUBLICATION DATA

Winward, Lane L.
    The healthy lawn handbook / Lane L. Winward.
      p. cm.
    Includes index.
    ISBN 1-55821-148-9
    1. Lawns—Handbooks, manuals, etc. I. Title.
  SB433.W49 1992
  635.9′647—dc20   92-2902
                                CIP

(M) 635.9642 W

THE COLLEGE of West Anglia

LANDBEACH ROAD • MILTON • CAMBRIDGE
TEL: (01223) 860701

13 MAR

0 1 MAY 2002

2 9 MAY 2002

2 6 MAR 2003

2 5 MAY 2005

2 3 JAN 20 WITHDRAWN

15/3/11

LEARNING *Centre*

The ticket - holder is responsible for
the return of this book

NORFOLK COLLEGE LIBRARY

3 8079 00055 319 8

Contents

Introduction

The Healthy Lawn Handbook has been designed to provide you with quick, useful information to help you care for your lawn. Most people who own a home have a lawn to take care of. The information provided here can take all the guesswork out of this task. You will discover how to raise your lawn to peak appearance and to maintain this appearance with the most up-to-date techniques. Few people have the time to gain the years of on-hand experience necessary to maintain beautiful grass. This book is intended to solve that problem.

1 🌾 Varieties of Grass

People grow lawns for many reasons. Lawns beautify the surroundings and help prevent soil erosion. In hot weather, they cool the air near the earth's surface. Lawns even reduce noise pollution by absorbing sound.

A successful lawn is one that grows evenly with uniform color and texture throughout.

There are many varieties of grass suitable for different climates. There are grasses that grow fast and some that grow slowly, grasses that have broad leaves and those of fine leaf texture. Some can be mowed short, others must be cut long. The following are some main lawn characteristics you should look for to plan your new lawn or improve an old one that exhibits problems:

Shade grass is for landscaped lawns that have an abundance of trees and/or areas that are shaded by buildings and fences. This grass makes do with little sunlight and is adept at fighting off mold and moss.

Sun grass is for lawn surfaces that will be subjected to direct sunlight for extended periods of time throughout the year. This grass sends down deep roots to reach and hold moisture and has blades capable of retaining water for longer periods without withering.

Dry area grass thrives in climates that have little annual rainfall, limited access to artificial watering systems, and hard, unirrigated soil.

Wet area grass will grow in dirt that is constantly moist or flooded. This grass fights mold and fungus well and is good at quickly dispersing water through evaporation and natural synthesis.

By planting and growing the particular strain that is best suited for your grounds, a healthy lawn is maintained. Many people are not aware of these subtle differences in lawn varieties so they plant a sun grass throughout a whole plot, not thinking that when the shade trees in one corner are grown the grass there will become sparse and die. Or sometimes they do the reverse with a shade strain or a water strain.

Expert advice is invaluable in choosing *what* grass is used *where* on your property. Considerable thought should also be spent deciding what other conditions a lawn will be subjected to. Will your lawn need to be durable to stand up to dogs and children, or will it be only for decoration and display? It is important to consult with a lawn specialist and plant accordingly to attain the maximum efficiency and beauty of the grass on your property.

MAKEUP OF A GRASS PLANT

A lawn is made up of many thousands of individual grass plants. These plants grow from the *crown*, which sprouts directly from the ground. When cutting a lawn, if the crown is not damaged your lawn will continue to grow with barely a halt. Underneath the crown is an underground network of roots. These roots take in water and nutrients, and they anchor the plant.

Reaching up from the crown is the *primary shoot*. This is the first stem that develops from a seeded grass plant. The primary shoot is made up of *blades, collar, sheath, nodes,* and *internodes.* A blade and sheath together make up a leaf. A band called the collar marks the spot where the blade and sheath come together.

Blades and sheaths come from rounded joints called nodes. The sections of stem between the nodes are called internodes. Blade shoots that grow out from the crown but are beside the primary shoot are called *tillers.* The presence of many tillers will make a lawn thick, lush, and full in appearance.

A grass plant, with its parts.

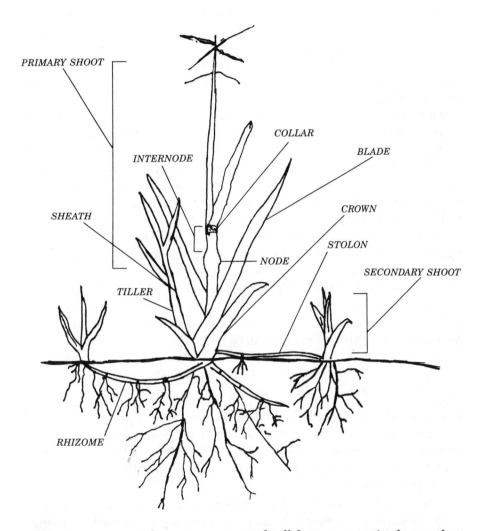

PRIMARY SHOOT
COLLAR
INTERNODE
BLADE
SHEATH
CROWN
STOLON
NODE
SECONDARY SHOOT
TILLER
RHIZOME

Bunch grasses, such as ryegrasses and tall fescues, grow in clumps that fill a lawn space. Creeping grasses spread by stems that reach out from the original plant. These stems are called *rhizomes* if they reach out below the ground, and *stolons* if they reach out above the ground. Some grasses spread by rhizomes only and some spread by stolons only. Other grasses spread by both stolons and rhizomes.

SPECIFIC GRASS STRAINS

Grasses are usually categorized as either *warm season* or *cool season*. Cool season grasses grow very well in high elevations in the South and nearly all elevations in the North. These lawns grow profusely in the cool weather of the spring and fall, and slowly in the heat of summer. With adequate watering, these grasses will remain green all year round. Kentucky bluegrass, bent grass, ryegrass, and fescues are examples of cool season grasses.

Warm season grasses grow best in the southern parts of the United States. They grow actively in the warm summer months and then become dormant when cold weather strikes. These grasses turn brown in the cold seasons and will not do well in cold climates. Bermuda grass, Bahia grass, centipede grass, St. Augustine grass, and zoysia grass are common warm season grasses. Warm season grasses that will tolerate cold climates are buffalo grass and blue grama.

In an effort to create more disease-resistant and hardier strains of grass, man has taken the basic strains and bred them together to create many different cultivated varieties. These *cultivars* are more resistant to insects and adverse growing conditions, and newer strains with better refinements and capabilities are created every year to replace the old cultivars. Thus, to solve a problem with a section that will not seem to support grass growth, perhaps a new cultivated variety can be researched to suit the needs of the difficult area.

The following are examples of different varieties of grasses and some of their characteristics:

Kentucky Bluegrass (cool season) is the most widely grown lawn grass. It is the principal variety in all good lawn mixtures. It is also frequently planted alone. Kentucky bluegrass thrives on most types of Western soils but is difficult to get started on heavily alkaline soils. Bluegrass also has many improved cultivars.

Sometimes Kentucky bluegrass suffers from summer heat or can be easily damaged by mowing too short. Fertilizer needs are medium to high and the cutting length should be from 1½ to 3 inches in summer.

Best areas for growth are the Sierra Nevada, the Rocky Mountains; the north-central and northeastern states; the higher mountains of the upper South.

Cultivated varieties include Adelphi, Baron, Bensun (A-34), Bristol, Challenger, Columbia, Eclipse, Fylking, Glade, Kenblue, Majestic, Midnight, Newport, Parade, Plush, Rugby, Sydsport, Touchdown, Victa.

Creeping Red Fescue, Red Fescue (cool season) is often a component of bluegrass mixtures. Fescues do what many others cannot do—grow well in shade or dry soil. It has a high tolerance to ground acid. Fertilizer needs are low to medium and mowing heights are 1½ to 2½ inches.

Some of the problems are susceptibility to summer diseases in hot, humid climates and slow recovery when damaged. The best regions for growth are where the summers are not very hot, such as as Oregon and other coastal northwest areas. They grow quite well in most of the Great Lakes region.

Some cultivars are Aurora, Banner, Boreal, Cascade, C-26, Dawson, Ensylva, Fortress, Highlight, Jamestown, Koket, Reliant, Scaldis, Shadow, Waldina.

Creeping Bent Grass (cool season) can grow in acid soil with poor drainage. This grass is used for golf-course putting greens, lawn bowling, and other similar types of lawns. Creeping bent must be cut quite low or it creates too much of a thatch layer. Similar to all bent grasses, creeping bent grass is susceptible to many diseases. It grows best in full sun with little shade.

Water needs are high for this grass and fertilizer needs are medium to high. Creeping bent grass grows best in the moist soils of the northern United States and Canada. Cultivars are Penncross, Emerald, Seaside, Prominent, Penneagle.

Common Bermuda Grass (warm season) grows best in warm, humid climates. It stays green for most months of the year. Bermuda is easy to grow in most soils and will handle considerable traffic without damage. It has low maintenance requirements. Mow 1 to 1½ inches.

Problems with common Bermuda grass are browning in the fall until spring and very low shade tolerance. Fertilizer needs are medium to high and watering requirements are low. The best places to plant are the lower elevations of the Southwest, Maryland to Florida, Kansas, Oklahoma, and Texas.

The only present cultivar is Arizona Common.

Improved Bermuda Grass (warm season) has most of the same good points of common Bermuda grass but grows softer, thicker, and more finely textured. In most cases, a shorter dormant period is experienced.

More water is needed and more mowing than common Bermuda grass, and perhaps even more thatch control. It will not grow in shade in most instances. Fertilizer needs are medium to high and traffic tolerance is excellent. Mow ½ to 1 inch in height.

Cultivars are Midway, Midiron, Ormond, Santa Ana, Tifdwarf, Tifgreen, Tifway, Tufcote, Vamont, Tifway II.

St. Augustine Grass (warm season) will grow in salty soil and does well in shade. Augustine is also extremely fast growing and hardy. Water needs are high and fertilizer needs are medium to high. Cinch bugs can do considerable damage and this grass tends toward heavy thatch. St. Augustine is also prone to SAD virus (grass decline). Mowing height should be 2 to 3 inches.

Best areas to plant are southern California, Hawaii, mild areas in the Southwest, and Gulf Coast states.

Cultivars are Bitter Blue and Floratam.

Bahia Grass (warm season) has low maintenance and extensive root systems. These root systems are a great help in erosion control and require lower amounts of water.

Bahia has coarse blades, however, and, being fast growing, it requires very frequent mowing to continue looking good. Fertilizer needs are medium. Mowing height should be 2 to 3 inches. The best regions in which to grow it are the central coast of North Carolina to eastern Texas. It grows well in Florida also.

Cultivars are Argentine and Pensacola.

Zoysia Grass (warm season) forms a dense, fine-textured lawn that fights back against weeds and has good tolerance to heat and drought. It is also disease- and insect-resistant.

Zoysia is very slow to establish and will not grow where summers are short or cool. It will build too much thatch if overfertilized or cut too long. Fertilizer needs are low to medium. Mowing height is 1 to 2 inches. It grows best in most southern climates.

Cultivars are Meyer, El Toro, Belair, Emerald, Manila.

Centipede Grass (warm season) is a good low-maintenance lawn. It lives well in poor soil and is hardy enough to crowd out weeds. It will require more mowing than most grasses.

Centipede is coarse textured, however, and is very light green and so does not appear as healthy as other strains. It is very sensitive to low temperatures and must be watched for thatch buildup. It has low fertilizer needs and should to be mowed 1 to 2 inches. It has a very shallow root system.

Centipede grows best in the Southern United States where there is high humidity. Cultivars are Centiseed, Oklawn, Centennial, Raleigh.

Grama Grass (warm season) is a nondecorative grass that is usually planted in rangeland or other never-watered situations. Grama is a native grass and can be difficult to find since there is little demand for its seeds. It has excellent heat tolerance and is good in arid and alkaline soils. It is not recommended for mowing areas. It has low fertilizer needs and grows best in the great plains, where it originates.

Turf-Type Perennial Ryegrass (cool season) has the trait of fast germination and establishment. It works well with many mixtures to create a fast growth for protection of finer strains that are slower growing. It has improved heat and cold tolerance along with resistance to heavy traffic.

Fertilizer needs are low to medium but water needs are high. Mowing height should be 1 to 2 inches. The best areas in which to grow it are coastal regions with mild winters and cool, moist summers.

Cultivars are All Star, Blazer, Citation II, Cowboy, Derby, Loretta, Manhattan II, Omega II, Palmer, Pennant, Penfine, Prelude, Premier, Regal.

Annual Ryegrass (cool season) is fast germinating and is often used as a temporary planting. It has poor heat and cold tolerance and does not mow well. Annual ryegrass gives protection for more permanent and hardy grasses to grow and establish but dies after one year, leaving these more permanent strains to flourish.

Fertilizer needs are low but watering needs are high. It should be mowed 1 to 2 inches.

Rough Bluegrass (cool season) grows well in wet, shady areas and so is a component of shady lawn mixtures. It has a shallow root system that will not tolerate dry weather. Water needs are high but fertilizer needs are low. It does not handle traffic well.

Mowing height should be 1 to 2 inches. The best areas for growth are the wet, shaded regions in the northern states. Cultivars are Sabre, Colt.

Hard Fescue and Chewings Fescue (cool season) have improved performance compared to other fine fescues because they have better resistance to heat, leaf spot, drought, red thread, and dollar spot. They grow well in the shade.

Hard fescue is slower to establish than other fine-textured lawns. Mowing height is 2 to 2½ inches and fertilizer needs are low. It grows best in regions where summer nighttime temperatures are moderate to fair.

Cultivars are the same as creeping red fescue.

2 ❦ Planting Grass

There are four types of planting procedures: *seeding, sodding, sprigging,* and *plugging*. Of the three, sodding is the most popular. With better techniques of sodding and seeding, sprigging has become seldom used except where where warm season grasses predominate. Some grasses (like hybrid Bermuda grass) do not produce viable seed and *must* be sprigged or plugged.

SEEDING

Seeding is the cheapest method of planting grass. The seeds can be distributed by hand on most sites, but for large areas you should use a push-type spreader. There is also the added option of *hydro-seeding,* a procedure performed by professionals. The best time to plant seed is in the early fall or early spring.

ULTRAGREEN SHADE

Ingredients	Purity	Germ	Origin
Red Fescue	48.94%	85%	Oregon
Chewings fescue	39.15%	85%	Oregon
Perrenial Ryegrass	9.79%	85%	Oregon
Inert matter	1.72%		
Weed seed	0.25%	Net WT	
Crop seed	0.15%	3 LBS	

Lot No. 12504-1zz   Date Tested   1-90

IN CALIFORNIA SELL BY 3-92

Noxious weeds: None Found

The SOD HEAD GRASS CO.
1234 Downtowne, U.S.A.   97218

This is a sample seed label that you will find on grass seed boxes, sacks, or containers. The portions of grass listed are only a sample. A good seed mixture is indicated by a low percentage of weed and crop seeds, an absence of noxious weeds and a high percentage of germination.

Sow half the seed by walking back and forth over the soil. Sow the other half by walking at right angles to the first direction. Cover the seed by raking the soil lightly, but do not bunch the seed. Roll the soil lightly to provide a compact surface.

You can cover the soil with a light layer of straw or even grass clippings

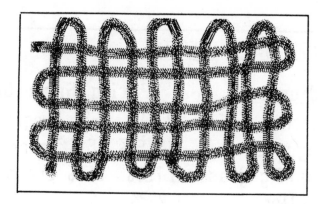

Sow seeed and spread fertilizer in the same pattern. Walk back and forth over the area with half of the total amount and spread the other half by walking back and forth at right angles.

from another lawn. This cover helps to hold in water, prevent erosion, and protect the seedlings from drying out. Water the soil lightly and often until the lawn has developed fairly well.

SODDING

This is usually the most effective and consequently the most expensive way to plant grass. Squares of soil already covered with grass are dug up (usually from sod farms) and placed over the soil of a lawn site. This method is most important to use on slopes that would erode easily if planted another way. There is less preparation and a site is provided with a viable growing lawn almost instantly.

SPRIGGING

This procedure involves the use of *sprigs,* small chunks or cuttings of grass. Sprigs are planted at intervals, depending on the variety of grass. As the sprigs grow, their low-lying stems creep along the ground and root in the soil, thus filling in the lawn site. Sprigging is extremely slow to create a whole lawn in comparison to the other techniques, so most people do not utilize this method, though the practice is still somewhat common in the Southern states.

PLUGGING

Plugs are made out of small squares or circles that are cut from sod and

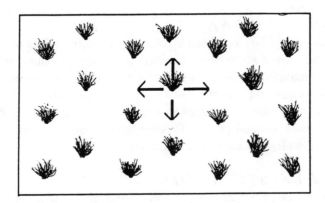

Sprigs are planted eight to ten inches apart and are copiously fertilized and watered. Sprig plantings are intended to spread in all directions and eventually fill in the entire planted area.

are planted 6 to 12 inches apart in much the same pattern as sprigging, and the grass will fill in a bit faster. Though they need to be kept moist, plugs will not dry out as fast as sprigs, lasting a day or two longer.

PLANTING PREPARATIONS

Much of the success in planting a lawn depends on how well the soil is prepared beforehand. Unlike a vegetable or flower garden, where the soil can be changed and built up each year, a lawn grows in the same soil year after year.

Although most nutrient deficiencies can be corrected after the lawn has been established, changing the soil texture under a growing lawn is difficult and quite expensive. The effort spent in preparing the soil will be rewarded by the health and beauty of your lawn for years to come. This is true for seed lawns as well as sod lawns. Even though sod has a little soil already attached, soil preparation is still very important to success.

PLAN AHEAD
Remove the top 6 inches of soil. Push it off to one side and save it for respreading. Remove any debris—plaster, stones, and trash; do not bury it. Fill any trenches or depressions with soil and thoroughly settle with water.

11

GRADE THE LAWN

The grade should be sloped slightly—away from the house—to carry off surplus water. Avoid steep slopes; gentle and smooth slopes are prettier and easier to maintain. A 1- to 1½-foot drop in 10 linear feet is excellent. For steeper grades, ground covers other than grass should be used.

Stay away from abrupt changes in grade that result in burned or dried spots and mower-scalped crests. To keep lawn areas at minimum grade, use retaining walls of concrete or oiled wood.

STUDY EXISTING SOIL

There are three principal types of soil—sand, clay, and loam. Sandy soil is made up of rather large particles. It drains easily but may lack humus, the organic matter in soil. Clay soil is made up of very fine particles of disintegrated rock. It holds tremendous quantities of water and frequently has poor drainage. Loamy soil is an easily crumbled mixture of different proportions of clay, sand, and organic matter. It is ideal for lawns.

If you have sandy or clay soil, there are many things you can do to change the physical characteristics of either one. Soil rebuilding with peat moss and commercial fertilizer is usually cheaper than excavating and refilling with new soil.

FERTILIZE YOUR SOIL

The best way to improve soil is to mix in (with the garden tool of your choice) as much organic fertilizer as possible. Leaves and grass and compost are best. Peat moss creates an ideal seed bed.

Don't waste humus by mixing it too deep. Stay within the top four or five inches. If your soil is extremely gravelly or filled with clay, or if it is necessary to raise the grade, then you will need to bring in some topsoil. Be careful to get only the best quality.

PREPARE THE SEED BED

After your grade has been established and your humus and fertilizer have been mixed into the soil, or following the spreading and improving of added topsoil, your area is ready for sodding or seeding.

If the previous steps have been done right this should be a simple job. Using a lawn rake, pull all high spots into the low spots until the surface is as smooth as possible. Rolling with a heavy roller at this stage will reveal any soft spots that would later sink and cause depressions. This is the time to install a sprinkler system.

To finish the lawn bed, remove all stones over an inch in diameter and,

The best way to even out a planting surface is to use a roller (usually filled with water for necessary weight) over the entire area to be planted.

with a rake, powder the soil into a fine uniform texture by breaking up all clods and smoothing the surface evenly. Rocks just under the surface cause the grass to dry in spots during hot weather. A smooth seed bed of uniform texture absorbs water evenly, insuring uniform germination of any seed and even growth of any grass. Eventually this also insures easier mowing.

PREVENT WEED GROWTH
This step can be eliminated if your soil is not badly contaminated with weed seeds. Different quantities of weed seeds occur in all soils. The annual weeds will die after several cuttings and do not usually come back. There are certain chemicals, however, that when applied can make your lawn weed-free from the start. Some of these are mentioned in a later chapter. For most correct applications, brands, and amounts, contact your local nursery experts.

SELECT A GOOD LAWN SEED/TURF
This may well be the most important decision you will make regarding your new lawn. It will certainly have the most far-reaching influence on lawn beauty and on its later maintenance requirements.

As was mentioned in the previous chapter, there are grasses that grow fast and those that grow more slowly. There are grasses for damp areas, shade, and direct sunlight. Examine your lawn and pick out the seed/turf that will grow best in each section.

Do not be afraid to have different varieties of grass in different areas of your yard. This is a necessary procedure for a successful lawn.

IF PLANTING—SOW THE SEED CORRECTLY

Grass seed can be spread either by hand or by a seeder. With either method of spreading seed, use a crisscross pattern to avoid spotty coverage. In this procedure you spread half of the seed amount while walking north and south, and the other half while walking east and west.

Cover the seed by lightly raking over the surface, and then, if a roller is available, roll lightly to press the seed gently into the soil. A one eighth-inch dressing of peat moss spread evenly over the surface will conserve moisture and ensure better, more even germination.

IF SODDING—LAY THE SOD CORRECTLY

The ground should be deeply watered for a week before laying the sod. Lay the sod in a bricklayer's pattern, making sure that the slanted edges are matched to fit evenly. If the edges are matched correctly, grass on the sod square edges will not die. Use a sharp sod-cutting tool to make the sod fit around obstructions. Do not be afraid to cut the sod. Just ensure that the edges are well matched.

When the sod is laid, lightly roll the entire surface to ensure evenness.

KEEP TRAFFIC OFF

It is important to keep traffic off a newly seeded or sodded lawn. If a fence is impractical, a humorous sign may help win cooperation. For example, you might write, "Your feet are killing me!"

A seeded lawn should have little or no traffic for at least a month. Sodded lawns should be protected for at least two weeks.

WATER FREQUENTLY

A lot of work and valuable sod or seed can be wasted and a lawn can be a complete failure unless adequate water is supplied frequently during the germination/rooting period.

Watering should be done slowly and lightly but must be often enough to avoid drying of the surface soil where the new tender roots and shoots are gaining a foothold. Early morning watering is best to keep the new grass and soil moist throughout the day.

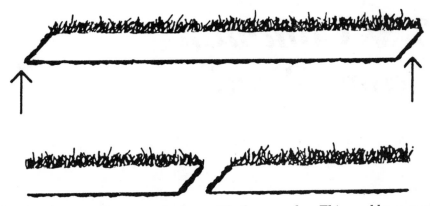

Good sod companies cut sod edges with these angles. This enables a good interlocking fit for sod placement.

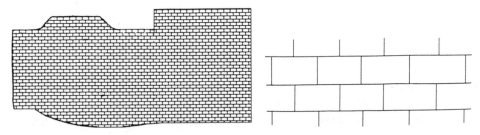

For best growth between edges, sod is placed in a bricklayer's pattern. This pattern should continue throughout, even when the laying area is not an equal-sided shape.

POINTS TO REMEMBER

- Your first cutting should not occur until the seeded or sodded lawn has reached a fairly uniform length of 3 inches.

- Very light amounts of fertilizer applied weekly will ensure continued food for a new lawn.

- Use extreme caution with weed killers in the first year. Hand remove any very troublesome weeds.

3 🌿 Common Lawn Weeds

A well-kept lawn seldom has weeds. The best long-range control measure for most lawn weeds starts with good fertilization, good watering procedures, and good lawn sanitation, so that permanent grasses get a head start on weeds.

Yet when weeds do take root by wind, lawn equipment, or organic matter and begin to spread, it is best to learn to recognize the weed and then seek professional advice on the best method of removal. This expert advice on the new weed controls that are constantly being developed can usually be obtained from your nearest nursery or garden supply center.

WEED CATEGORIES

Weeds are categorized according to several traits. First, they are either perennials or annuals. Perennials are those that live for two or more years. Annual weeds are those that live only one year. Weeds are further categorized by their leaf types—broad-leaved or narrow-leaved. Those that are broad-leaved have easily observed flowers and their leaves have a pattern of small veins that sometimes divide the leaves in half; an example would be thistle. An example of narrow-leaved would be grasses, which have hollow stems and long, narrow leaf blades with parallel veins. Another, much less common weed group is sedges. In appearance like grasses, they have triangular stems.

COMMON WEEDS TO WATCH FOR

Clover (annual, broad-leaved) has several different varieties. White clover and Burclover are the problem varieties in most lawns. Clover forms thick patches that choke out grass, but is mostly undesirable because of the uneven appearance created in an otherwise smooth lawn.

No preemergence controls. Postemergence should incorporate a product containing dicamba or MCPP in spring or late fall.

Crab Grass (annual, narrow-leaved) is noted for its broad blades and rough texture. Crabgrass begins in early spring and grows fast until the seed head forms in summer or early fall. Preemergent weed killers must be applied in the spring before seedlings appear. Chemicals that work best contain benefin, bensulide, DCPA, oxadiazon, pendimethalin, or siduron.

For postemergence control use arsenicals such as MSMA or MAMA. For best results apply these when the weeds are small. If needed, repeat treatment after seven to ten days or as instructions on the product label allow.

Clover has many varieties. White clover is the problem variety— this weed forms thick patches that choke out grass.

Crabgrass has broad blades and is rough textured. It is sometimes called "Orchard grass."

Dandelion (perennial, broad-leaved) has a bright yellow flower that soon brings a halo of seeds to scatter in the wind. This weed sends down a root sometimes as far as a foot and a half and if only 2 inches of the root survives a removal, it is enough for the plant to continue to grow. It grows best in spring and fall. As yet no preemergence chemicals are on the market for home use, but new ones are being developed.

For postemergence control, 2,4-D and MCPP are most effective. Spray on a windless day when temperatures are higher than 60 degrees but less than 85 degrees Fahrenheit.

Dandelions spread fast and easily. To get rid of a plant the entire root must be eliminated.

Dock (perennial, broad-leaved) looks somewhat similar to dandelion, but the leaves are less green and glossy and have a "twisted" appearance.

The best season of growth is spring. There are no preemergence controls. For postemergence use 2,4-D or dicamba.

Ground Ivy (perennial, broad-leaved) has leaves that are rounded like a kidney and tube-shaped flowers that are purple or blue. This trailing plant has creeping stems that form thick masses wherever they get a foothold.

It grows well in spring, summer, and fall. No preemergence controls are available as yet. Postemergence controls are 2,4-DP or 2,4-D during spring or
fall.

Henbit (annual, broad-leaved) has a four-sided stem and is a variety of the mint family. The best growth is during the spring and fall. Preemergence controls do not yet exist for home use. Postemergence controls are dicamba, MCPP, or 2,4-D. Two applications may be required.

Knotweed (annual, broad-leaved) grows particularly in hard, compacted soils. Aeration will help eliminate it as a problem. It grows best in early spring through early fall.

Preemergence controls are not yet available for home use. For postemergence use dicamba or MCPP. Treatments should be applied anytime during the active growth of early spring.

Mallow (annual, broad-leaved) is often called cheeseweed, gets started in early spring, and has a long growing season. There are not yet any pre-

Ground Ivy has leaves that are shaped like a kidney. This trailing plant has creeping stems that form thick masses.

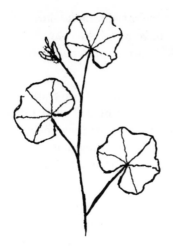

Mallow grows from several stems, but has one deep—and very difficult to remove—main root. This plant is sometimes called "cheeseweed."

emergence controls. Postemergence controls are dicamba, MCPP, or 2,4-D. Spray from mid to late spring.

Mouse-Ear Chickweed (perennial, broad-leaved) has very small leaves that are usually extremely dark green. It grows fast and plentiful in the cool weather of spring and fall.

No preemergence herbicides are presently available for home use. Postemergence controls are dicamba or MCPP. Apply these chemicals during spring or fall when temperatures are between 60 degrees and 70 degrees Fahrenheit.

Oxalis (perennial, broad-leaved) grows best in spring and late fall. It looks similar to clover and henbit, but its leaves are more fragile and light green than either.

There are no preemergence controls. Postemergence controls are products with dicamba, MCPP, 2,4-D, or 2,4-DP. Apply in the spring or fall when the temperature is at least 60 degrees but no more than 80 degrees Fahrenheit. Several treatments are usually required.

Plantain (perennial, broad-leaved) is a group low-growing herbs, several of which are common weeds that invade lawns. They have a circular cluster of bright green leaves that grow directly from the roots. Tall, slender spikes grow up from the center of the cluster.

Plantains grows best in cool seasons. No preemergence controls are yet developed for home use. Postemergence controls are MCPP or 2,4-D, to be applied before the center spikes sprout.

Plantains have fleshy leaves sent up from one root system and stem. Seed stems must not be allowed to grow.

Purslane (annual, broad-leaved) looks similar to spurge but has thicker leaves that are glossy in appearance and rubbery in texture. It grows all summer long.

For preemergence use DCPA applied from early spring to midspring. For postemergence use dicamba or 2,4-D from mid to late summer.

Spurge (annual, broad-leaved) has small inconspicuous flowers called *bracts* (leaves that look like flower petals) and a biting milky juice. There are 7,300 species in this family of herbs, which does include some shrubs and trees.

Purslane has glossy green leaves with one stem and many branches.

Spotted spurge has one main root growing straight down, yet the plant itself sends out long branches with many tiny leaves.

Spurge grows fastest in late spring and early fall. For preemergence use DCPA or siduron in spring before germination. For postemergence use dicamba or 2,4-D. These may require two applications.

Thistle (perennial, broad-leaved) is a group of plants that have sharp spines or prickles. The two North American varieties are *tall thistle* and *pasture thistle*. These plants are characterized by tough fibrous stems, prickly leaves with many lobes, and soft, silky flowers that are usually purple or pinkish.

Thistle grows best during the cool weather of spring and fall. Preemergence controls do not exist at this time. Of postemergence controls

Thistles are characterized by tough, fibrous stems, prickly leaves, and purple or pinkish flowers.

2,4-D works best. Spray in the fall; two applications may be needed. Spot apply only with glyphosate.

Tree Saplings Certain trees propagate by sending out roots—sometimes up to a hundred feet—that push up shoots to form saplings. A good example is the mountain west poplar variety called *Quaking Aspen.* When one of this kind of tree borders a lawn, the saplings can be quite bothersome. And if they are just cut off every week with a mower, a hard knot or blister of wood forms.

There are no preemergence controls. For postemergence, use glyphosate for spot contact. In some instances cacodylic acid will work with spot application.

Veronica (annual, broad-leaved), also called speedwell, is very low lying, has tiny light blue flowers and tiny green leaves, and is very tough to kill. There are several barely varying species. Seed pods are heart shaped. It grows best in spring and fall.

There are no preemergence controls available. For postemergence use 2,4-D in the fall or DCPA at the flowering time in the spring. Two or more applications may be needed.

WEED CONTROL

There are four general methods of weed control—*cultural, mechanical, biological,* and *chemical.*

Cultural control is the use of efficient lawn variety to prevent weeds from growing. Also included is the technique of planting grass in an area that has been made weed free by the use of a mulch, grass clippings, or plastic sheeting.

Mechanical control is the destruction of weeds manually or by a machine. Many weeds can be removed by hand; these are weeds with shallower root systems. Others can be removed with the help of tools that can reach down deep and remove a long root entirely. Sometimes a specific technique of mowing will kill a weed in a lawn.

Biological control involves the use of natural enemies of weeds growing in a specific area. For example, insects and other small animals that eat certain weeds may be put into a lawn where those weeds are growing. Bacteria and other organisms can be used to spread diseases among specific species of weeds. Sometimes a certain amount of watering is an enemy to a weed, depending on the area and species of the weed.

Chemical control is the use of chemical compounds called herbicides. Most herbicides are selective—that is, they kill weeds but do not harm the grass, human beings, or wildlife.

Many, however, are not selective. They can only be sprayed directly on the plant and must not be touched by humans or animals for a measured amount of time. These non-selectives seem to work the best for removal of troublesome weeds in grass, but must be painstakingly applied to each individual weed.

Following is a list of herbicides that can be applied to rid weeds from a patch of ground *before* planting:

Atrazine controls several annual grasses and broad-leaved weeds, but only in lawns of centipede grass, St. Augustine grass, or zoysia grass. It does not do damage to woody ornamental plants.

Benefin will control annual grasses in many lawns, but is not safe for bent grasses. It prevents all seeds from germinating for about eight weeks.

Bensulide is a control for annual grasses and certain broad-leaved weeds. Seeds will not grow for four months after an application. It is safe for use on bent-grass lawns.

DCPA is especially deadly to germinating seeds of certain broad-leaved species, including chickweed and purslane. This is damaging to new lawns, and reseeding cannot be done for eleven to thirteen weeks. It is not recommended for bent grass.

Oxadiazon controls annual grasses. Do not use on fine fescue or bent grass. Do not reseed for at least four months.

Pendimethalin is used for many annual grasses and some broad-leaved weeds. It is not recommended for bent grass.

Siduron works well on weedy grasses, including crabgrass, foxtail, and barnyard grass. Siduron has the unique trait of not interfering with the germination of cool season grasses such as Kentucky bluegrass.

Following is a list of herbicides that are applied *after* planting:

CAMA, MAMA, MSMA are a group of chemicals called organic arsenicals.

They control grassy weeds like crabgrass and foxtail. They are effective against some nutsedges. More than one application is required.

Cacodylic acid kills only on contact. Repeat treatments are needed to kill hardy perennials. This chemical works by killing all green growing leaf tissue. It will not move through a plant to the root system. It is also sometimes used to clear weeds from an area prior to planting a lawn.

Dalapon is used against all grasses. Spot treatment is the most efficient and effective method of application. Residual toxicity can last for four months.

Dicamba is frequently used against clover, chickweed, and knotweed. Dicamba affects plant hormones. It is absorbed through the roots and leaves. Do not use where roots of desirable plants may run under the area to be treated.

Glyphosate is nonselective and systemic, meaning it kills both grasses *and* broad-leaved weeds. It is an effective chemical for most perennial grassy weeds.

MCPP is similar to 2,4-D but is safer to use on new lawns or sensitive grasses such as bent grass or St. Augustine grass.

2,4-D is available in many forms. It is a growth-influencing hormone that affects broad-leaved weeds in a lawn and kills them. This herbicide works with little damage to most existing lawns.

2,4-DP is very similar to 2,4-D. It controls hard-to-kill broad-leaved weeds. Some examples are oxalis and mugwort.

Remember: New weed controls are constantly being developed. Keep in touch with your local garden supply dealer for the most up-to-date advice.

4 🌿 *Lawn Diseases*

Various diseases affect grass and thrive in different climates. It can be extremely difficult to diagnose a problem because many of the characteristics of a lawn disease are similar to other problems, such as tree roots under a lawn or a poor watering program. Or perhaps one of these conditions is the direct cause of a recurring disease.

To help eliminate many problems that cause diseases, it is necessary to follow a few simple rules of good lawn care.

- Plant a grass type that is adapted to your climate *and* landscaped area.

- Fertilize on a regular schedule that fits your lawn growth and grass type.

- Water for long periods on a regular schedule to allow grass roots to seek deeper for moisture.

- Mow at the proper height for your lawn. Remember that if a lawn is cut longer, it is more likely to be healthier.

- Aerate on a regular basis—no less than once a year, no more than three times a year (spring, summer, fall).

• Power rake to remove thatch whenever needed (when thatch is one-third inch or more deep).

If these measures are taken and a serious disease still takes hold, chemical control may be necessary. Most diseases may be controlled with chemicals, but some, such as stripe smut fungus, can be controlled only by planting disease-resistant grass. Analyze and identify the disease before taking measures for removal.

SOME COMMON DISEASES

BROWN PATCH

Description: Large, irregular, circular areas up to several feet in diameter. The spots are usually brown to gray in color and have a water-soaked appearance around the edges. These signs are usually only seen on leaves and stems.

Most affected grasses: Centipede grass, St. Augustine grass, Bermuda grass, bent grass, ryegrass, and zoysia grass.

Cultural control: Do not overdose with nitrogen. Aerate and water deeply. Remove causes of excess shade. Power rake whenever minimum need arises.

Chemical control: Use anilazine, benomyl, chlorothalonil, fenarimol, thiophanates, or triadimefon.

Brown patch is shown here as it affects a large surface. The appearance is similar to that of fertilizer burn.

COTTONY BLIGHT

Description: Sometimes this disease is called grease spot blight. It can affect an area a few inches or several feet in diameter. The diseased area will be surrounded by blackened blades covered with a white or gray mildew. Dry weather will halt the disease.

Most affected grasses: bent grass, Bermuda grass, ryegrass, and fescues.

Cultural control: Aerate profusely. Avoid watering heavily. Do not use excessive fertilizer.

Chemical control: Apply fungicides like propamocarb, etridiazole, chloroneb, or metalaxyl.

DOLLAR SPOT

Description: A fungus that attacks several different varieties of grass, it kills in small spots that are 3 to 12 inches in diameter. Many spots can, however, come together to form a large dead area. Affected areas usually range in color from dark tan to light yellow.

Most affected grasses: Bermuda grass, all fescues, Kentucky bluegrass, and ryegrass.

Cultural control: Use larger amounts of nitrogen. Aerate and water for longer periods. Decrease thatch through hand or mechanical means.

Chemical control: Use anilazine, benomyl, chlorothalonil, fenarimol, iprodione, thiophanates, triadimefon.

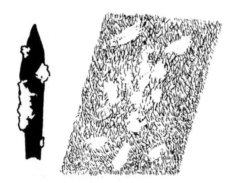

Typhula blight grows on individual blades of grass in this form and causes a damage pattern to an entire area.

Dollar spot affects grass blades in this pattern.

FAIRY RINGS

Description: Indicated by rings or arcs of dark green, fast-growing grass from several inches to over 40 feet. Fairy rings expand outward at a rate of anywhere from 2 inches to 4 feet per year. Rings may spring up as a result of buried organic matter such as lumber, logs, roots, or stumps, and are produced by any one of over fifty different kinds of fungus.

Most affected grasses: all grasses.

Cultural control: Apply increased nitrogen to hide the problem. Aerate profusely. Keep area wet for about two weeks and mow frequently. If this does not work, replace the soil to a depth of twelve inches or more and sod.

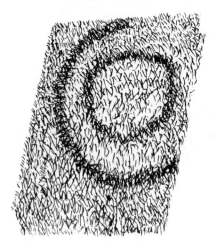

Fairy rings are usually caused by organic matter under the surface of a lawn. There can be a single such ring, or up to three or more.

Chemical control: There are no easy-to-use or entirely adequate chemicals to recommend at the time of this writing.

FUSARIUM PATCH

Description: Sometimes called pink snow mold, this disease most often develops under snow but can occur when no snow is present. Can be identified by white or pink circular patches that are 1 to 8 inches in diameter.

Most affected grasses: Kentucky bluegrass, creeping bent grass, ryegrass, and zoysia grass.

Cultural control: Decrease amount of shade in the affected area. Aerate well. Avoid any thatch buildup. Do not overfertilize.

Chemical control: Use applications of benomyl, fenarimol, mancozeb, or triadimefon.

LEAF SPOTS

Description: Indicated by purplish black, dark reddish brown, chocolate brown, light gray, or tan spots on leaves and stems. The spots can be round or oblong and may cause entire colonies of grass to turn yellow. Turf becomes thin, weak, or dying out in round to irregular spots that enlarge during summer months.

Most affected grasses: Delta, Kenblue, and Park Kentucky bluegrass.

Cultural control: Reduce the amount of shade. Improve aeration for better water drainage. Mow at top limit of cutting height.

Gray leaf spot affects blades in this pattern.

Chemical control: Apply anilazine, mancozeb, captan, iprodione, chlorothalonil, or cycloheximide.

MOSSES

Description: These occur in lawns that are low in nutrients and fertility with poor drainage, high acidity, too much shade, improper watering, or a combination of these. They appear as light green to dark, fuzzy or slimy growths that cover soil, grass, or objects such as rocks and garden ornaments.

Most affected grasses: all grasses where the above-mentioned conditions predominate.

Cultural control: Aerate well, rake affected area, remove causes of excess shade, use fertilizer such as amonium sulfate.

Chemical control: Use maneb, mancozeb, or wettable sulfur. These solutions are only temporary. Cultural control to eliminate the cause is the only permanent solution.

POWDERY MILDEW

Description: These mildews grow when nights are cool and days are warm. They occur mostly on bluegrasses and fescues. The mildew color is white, gray-white, and brown. Patches can be seen on leaves in shaded or poorly drained areas. The leaves can possibly yellow and wither. This is most serious on new plantings.

Most affected grasses: Bermuda grass, Kentucky bluegrass, and zoysia grass.

Cultural control: Remove causes of excess shade. Do not overwater and frequently aerate well. Do not overfertilize.

Chemical control: Benomyl, cycloheximide, or triadimefon.

RED THREAD

Description: Sometimes this disease is called Pink Patch. It affects mostly fescues, bent, and bluegrasses. Irregularly shaped pink patches of dead grass 2 to 6 inches or more in diameter develop during cool, damp weather in spring, fall, and winter. Usually only leaves are affected. If the disease is very severe, patches turn brown and die. Characteristic: coral-pink threads bind leaves together.

Most affected grasses: Kentucky bluegrass, red fescue, and ryegrass.

Cultural control: Use more nitrogen.

Chemical control: Anilazine, chlorothalonil, iprodione, mancozeb, or triadimefon.

RUST

Description: This problem is indicated by orange, reddish-brown, yellow, or black powdery deposits on leaves and leaf sheaths. If severe, leaves may yellow, wither, and die. Grass may be thinned, weakened, and more susceptible to drought, winter injury, and other diseases.

Most affected grasses: Kentucky bluegrass and ryegrass. All commonly grown grasses are susceptible.

Chemical control: Apply anilazine, chlorothalonil, cycloheximide, maneb, or triadimefon.

SLIME MOLDS

Description: They occur in warm weather following heavy watering or rains. Small white, gray, or yellow slimy masses that grow up and over grass surfaces in round to irregular patches, shading or discoloring otherwise healthy turf. Masses dry to form bluish, gray, yellow, black, or white powdery growths.

Most affected grasses: common Kentucky bluegrass, zoysia grass, bent grass, and fescue.

Cultural control: Aerate profusely. Dethatch even if thatch layer is less than one-third inch. Cut grass to lowest limit of height for your recommended variety.

Chemical control: Use benomyl, fenarimol, or triadimefon.

STRIPE SMUT

Description: Long or short stripes in leaves that rupture and release dark brown or black powdery masses. Sometimes leaves are shredded, wilted, and withered. Grass can yellow and later die in patches 2 to 8 inches in diameter.

Most affected grasses: bent grass and Kentucky bluegrass.

Cultural control: Do not overwater. Aerate regularly and keep thatch to a minimum.

Chemical control: Use PCNB, thiophanates, or triadimefon.

Stripe smut can take over large areas of a lawn. Long black stripes are seen on ruptured blades.

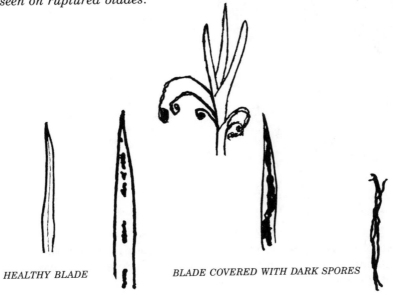

HEALTHY BLADE

BLADE COVERED WITH DARK SPORES

BEGINNING SMUT PATCHES

BLADE SHRIVELS AND DIES

SUMMER PATCH

Description: Sometimes called fusarium blight, summer patch starts out as light green patches that are ½ inch to 8 inches in diameter. These turn tan or reddish brown. When the patches are large, a characteristic called "frog eye" occurs. This is where a healthy-appearing patch of grass is partially surrounded by a ring of dead grass.

Most affected grasses: Kentucky bluegrass, perennial ryegrass, and tall fescues.

Cultural control: Frequent light watering helps during drought. Mow in medium range of height recommended for your grass variety.

Chemical control: Benomyl, iprodione, thiophanates, fenarimol, or triadimefon.

All in all, there are over twenty-one lawn disease groups that contain over a hundred different specific ailments. Also, some individual diseases are known by different names in different areas, making the specific mention of each and every disease or ailment impossible to place in this work.

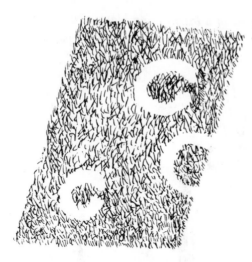

Here summer patch disease is shown in the frog-eye pattern. The affected areas are usually brown or dull tan.

Using the above-mentioned general descriptions, however, you can get a closer idea of which ailment could be affecting your lawn and thus take appropriate measures. As in all lawn problems, the advice of a professional has no substitute.

DAMAGE CAUSED BY NEGLECT

At times there are ailments that appear to be caused by disease but in fact are due to deficiencies in lawn care. It is important to be able to recognize these first, since the resulting difficulties are more easily straightened out.

CHEMICAL BURN

Description: Lawns damaged by dog defecation, spilled or overapplied fertilizer or herbicides, or gasoline, are characterized by round to irregular patches of dead yellow grass that will eventually (if not treated) blow and wash away to leave patches of bare soil.

Treatment: In the case of dog defecation and fertilizer burn, completely soak the soil with water. New seeds or grass sod replacements will be necessary for a quick cure.

In the case of gasoline or herbicide burn, soak the damaged area with soapy water that is about the consistency of dishwater. Then rinse completely with plain water. These bare patches will fill in from one to three months. The only quick cure is still seeding or sodding.

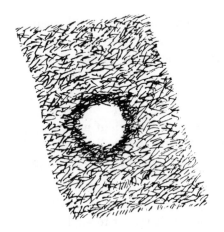

Fertilizer burn and dog-defecation problems appear very similar. The edges of the dead areas will be very green and seem more healthy than the normal grass because of the abundance of food.

Chemical burn creates a dead area. The spots look similar to a fertilizer burn but the edges will not be green.

DULL MOWER AND SCALPING

Description: Cutting your lawn with a dull blade gives it a grayish cast one or two days after it is mowed. This occurs because the grass is shredded instead of being cleanly cut. Then the shreds turn brown. Shredded tips allow easy entry for many diseases.

Scalping occurs when too much lawn (more than one-third reduction in height) is cut off at one time. The lawn will turn brown and sparse. This should not be mistaken for disease damage.

Treatment: The cures for these problems are simple and logical. Raise the height of your mower blade a half inch or more from the present height to prevent scalping, and buy a new blade or sharpen the old one to prevent shredding.

NITROGEN OR IRON DEFICIENCY
Description: Nitrogen is the largest-quantity nutrient needed by grass. If not enough nitrogen has been applied, your lawn will be yellowish and will not grow very well. If nitrogen is applied and it still does not grow and stays yellow, the difficulty can be lack of iron.

Treatment: Using a normal fertilizer on a lawn that needs iron will actually cause the grass to become yellower. It is best to apply both nitrogen and iron in tandem—apply them in a fertilizer that contains both.

SUMMER DRY SPOTS
Description: Hard, dry soil is a problem with all grasses. This problem occurs most often when the spring has been very wet and then summer heat follows closely or immediately behind. The grass becomes used to the continued moisture and only seeks water from the surface. When the heat arrives, the surface water dries up quickly and the lawn develops spots of brown grass, thin yellowish blades, and apparent areas of soil showing through sparse growths of grass.

Treatment: Plan a specific program of watering. Be certain that all areas of grass are covered and overlapped by any existing sprinkler system. If all areas are not covered sufficiently, a portable hose may be needed to water in dry areas.

LAWN FUNGICIDES

There are two basic types of fungicide. *Systemic,* which gets inside of a plant to kill a disease, and *nonsystemic,* which kills disease on the outside of plants. Systemic fungicides work the best, but they are selective—they only kill certain diseases. Nonsystemic fungicides are usually applied as a preventive measure.

Anilazine is nonsystemic. It is used against brown patch, typhula blight, rust, dollar spot, leaf spot, and red thread.

Benomyl is systemic. It is used against brown patch, fusarium patch, dollar spot, summer patch, and powdery mildew.

Captan is nonsystemic. It is used against most leaf spots.

Chloroneb is nonsystemic. It is used against pythium blight.

Chlorothalonil is nonsystemic. It is used against brown patch, rust, dollar spot, leaf spot, and red thread.

Cycloheximide is nonsystemic. It is used against leaf spot, powdery mildew, and rust.

Fenarimol is systemic. It is used against brown patch, typhula blight, fusarium patch, dollar patch, and summer patch.

Iprodione is systemic. It is used against brown patch, summer patch, red thread, typhula blight, dollar patch, and fusarium patch.

Mancozeb is nonsystemic. It is used against red thread, leaf spot, and fusarium patch.

Maneb is nonsystemic. It is used against rust and some leaf spots.

Metalxyl is systemic. It is used against cottony blight.

PCNB is partially systemic. It is used against stripe smut and some leaf spots.

Propamocarb is systemic. It is used against cottony blight.

Thiophanates is systemic. It is used against summer patch, brown patch, stripe smut, and dollar spot.

Triadimefon is systemic. It is used against dollar spot, brown patch, red thread, rust, fusarium patch, powdery mildew, stripe smut, summer patch, and typhula blight.

Note: New fungicides are being developed on a regular basis. It cannot be stressed enough how important it can be to keep in close touch with a professional nursery person to keep updated on the products that might be used for a problem occurring on your lawn.

5 🌿 *Lawn Pests*

Many kinds of insects and pests live in grass and lawns. Some are visible and some are far too small to be seen. Some are bothersome to lawn owners because of annoyance but do little or no actual damage to grass; others can obliterate a healthy lawn.

Unfortunately, many of the characteristics of a lawn damaged by insects or pests are exactly the same as those of a lawn damaged by disease or neglect. Thus diagnosing can be quite difficult.

One of the best, most simple methods of determining whether suspected insects or pests are present is by simple observation. In many cases, if a lawn has been damaged by a pest or insect enough to be noticed, the organism can easily be sighted. In the following pages of this chapter, descriptions and characteristics of many lawn pests are listed.

TYPES OF INSECT DAMAGE

There are three basic categories of insects that damage grass. One is the insect that lives above ground and sucks the plant juice. The second is the kind that lives below the surface and feeds on roots. And the third is the insect that lives at the soil surface and feeds on the grass blades.

The symptom of the first category is seen by the grass blades thinning out and turning brown. Whole patches dead and dying in round to irregular shapes can appear.

The symptom of category two is that blades turn yellow and die in irregularly shaped patches. When a person takes a handful of grass in these damaged areas, blades will come free and lightly out of the grass without any roots attached.

Category three's symptoms are quite noticeable. Round bare areas can appear, with the grass chewed right down to root level.

LAWN INSECTS

Armyworms chew off the grass blades from below the surface and cause round, bare areas in a lawn. If there are many armyworms present, the grass will be chewed off right to the soil level. Armyworms are yellowish white and have an upside-down Y on their heads.

For chemical control use acephate, diazinon, chlorpyrifos, or carbaryl.

Billbugs feed on grass roots and cause small circular patterns that turn yellowish and brown. Dead sections of grass will lift away easily from soil. There are many different species of billbugs that attack different varieties of grass.

For chemical control use diazinon.

Billbugs (here shown in larval stage and adult stage) feed on roots and stems.

Chiggers are actually mites. They wait for any animal or person to pass by to allow them to spread to different areas.

Chiggers do not do much damage to a lawn, but they are an extreme nuisance to lawn owners. They are not insects, but are spider mites that lay their eggs in soil. After hatching, the larvae crawl onto grass blades and latch on to any passing person or animal.

For chemical control use diazinon or chlorpyrifos.

Cinch Bugs damage lawns by sucking the juice directly from the leaves. Generally these insects are widespread and can be discovered upon close examination of grass blades that have turned yellow in distinct circular patches. They particularly enjoy St. Augustine grass, but Kentucky bluegrass and bent grass are affected also.

For chemical control use propoxur, isophenphos, diazinon, chlorpyrifos, or NPD.

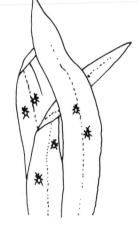

Cinch bugs suck juice directly from grass leaves. Generally these insects are widespread and can be discovered by examining individual blades.

Crane Flies lay eggs that produce grubs that feed on grass blades. This causes patches of grass to disappear, usually from the edge of the lawn. Sometimes a brownish paste will cover an area with a large concentration. Crane fly grubs are brown-gray and about an inch long.

For chemical control use diazinon.

Cutworms are extremely difficult to spot, not only because they live and stay far down in the root system, but because the appearance of the damage they cause is similar to that of so many other diseases and ailments. Cutworms eat the tender roots of the plant and this causes dead brown spots to form in round and irregular patches. If a person were to spill gas or use too much fertilizer in an area, the effect would be the same as the damage done by cutworms.

For chemical control use acephate, carbaryl, diazinon, or chlorpyrifos.

Greenbugs suck juice from the grass blades and at the same time inject a poison into the plant. They cause rust-colored patches of grass that turn brown and die. These patches start under trees and spread to sunnier sections of lawn. Greenbugs are very small aphids that like many grasses but seem to prefer Kentucky bluegrass.

For chemical control use acephate.

Grubs feed by sucking juices from and eating the roots of grass plants. They can be difficult to diagnose because of their location down in the sod that they dwell in. Also, there are hundreds of different kinds of grubs that will live in a lawn at different times of the year and in different stages of

Cut worms can be seen by removing sod from a small area. They are sometimes found curled up in round balls. The winged form is also shown.

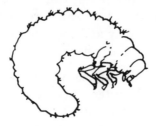

Grubs are the larvae stage of many different types of insects. They live in lawn-root systems.

development. Indications are brown patches, irregularly shaped, and affected sections will roll back similar to a carpet.

For chemical control use trichlorfon, chlorpyrifos, diazinon, or iso-phenphos.

Mole Crickets eat grass roots and cause irregular streaks of brown and wilted grass. Dead and dying grass will pull up very easily. Tunnels can be easily seen if the ground is bare. Mole crickets are about 2 inches long and are brown or gray in color.

For chemical control use propoxur and diazinon.

Root-Feeding Nematodes feed on lawn roots and cause grass to be slow growing and to not respond normally to watering and fertilizing. Often the grass looks stunted and yellowed with dead and dying areas. Sometimes this problem is confused with fertilizer burn, soil deficiency, and poor aeration. The grass roots may be missing, swollen, stunted, bushy, and dark in color.

There are many thousands of kinds of nematodes, but only a few are damaging to lawns. Complete diagnosis will require the assistance of a competent nematologist. Likewise, for control, only a professional should complete any kind of necessary application.

Sod Webworms live in the grass root system, but they surface to devour leaves and stems with an unstoppable hunger. Dead patches from 1 to 2 inches in diameter appear inside otherwise healthy, normally growing grass. Many birds feeding regularly on the lawn can indicate a high concentration of this insect. Sod worms are not as easy to spot as cinch bugs,

Sod webworms live in the roots but devour leaves. They are difficult to see but can be found by searching a grass clod.

but they can be discovered by examining a few two-inch clods of grass taken from various portions of a suspected area of lawn.

For chemical control use carbaryl, chlorpyrifos, diazinon, acephate, isophenphos, propoxur, NPD, or trichlorfon.

INSECTICIDES

When it becomes necessary to use an insecticide as a pest control, it is very wise to be extremely careful in reading *all* instructions on the label and taking any advice that can be garnered from a local professional gardener or nursery person.

Acephate is used for armyworms, greenbugs, and sod webworms.

Carbaryl has many forms, varieties, and uses. Manufacturers use it to control several different insects such as cutworms, cinch bugs, and sod webworms.

Chlorpyrifos is used on cinch bugs, sod webworms, and grubs.

Diazinon is used for many different insects, but works best for long-term control of grubs. It comes in many forms and is made by many different manufacturers.

Isophenphos is used for cinch bugs, mole crickets, grubs, and sod webworms.

NPD is used for cinch bugs and sod webworms. It lasts for up to eight weeks.

Propoxur is used on cinch bugs, earwigs, and leafhoppers. It is often seen in insect baits.

Trichlorfon is used for grubs, sod webworms, and mole crickets.

Note: It is important to remember that a well-maintained lawn will discourage even pesky insects. Though it will not keep them away completely, a healthy lawn will not be damaged as much as an unhealthy one. It will have higher resistance to pests and bounce back much faster after treatment.

6 ❧ *Watering*

PROCEDURES

In some climates watering of lawns is unnecessary because of normal rainfall. Even during dry periods these lawns should be watered only a couple of times weekly. Daily watering may cause weeds or weedy grasses to grow more rapidly than the lawn grass itself.

But for the many climates that are *dry* and require considerable amounts of watering, much time and a lot of money on water bills can be saved if certain recommendations are closely adhered to.

WATER DEPTH

Water should be penetrating soil to a depth of 6 to 12 inches or more. Under trees, water should soak down to a depth of 2 to 4 feet in order to insure that tree roots continue feeding in their natural zone and out of competition with a lawn. This deep watering encourages food- and moisture-seeking grass roots to reach farther down. Deeper root systems mean thicker and more beautiful lawns.

It takes one inch of measured water to penetrate 6 to 12 inches in the average soil mix. To cover 1,000 square yards with one inch of water takes 624 gallons, or 83 cubic feet.

SOIL TIMING

Timing will be different for various types of soil. You can figure that if sandy soil requires twenty minutes to soak one foot deep, loam would require thirty minutes. Under the same conditions clay would take about fifty minutes or more. It is important for clay soils not to be left dry for long periods because the hot sun can bake the clay soil almost rock hard.

NIGHT WATERING

It is best to water after the daylight hours because during even just a warm day over 30 percent of the sprinkled water will evaporate before penetrating the soil. If the day is very hot, an even higher percentage will just melt away.

During the cooler temperatures of nighttime, water can soak through a soil and stay present for hours longer than during the day. This allows a lawn to drink for longer periods and to stockpile moisture against the coming heat. Of all times, very late evenings or extremely early mornings are best for good watering. Quite often a person will find water pressure much higher at this time because of less home use.

HEAVY SPRINKLING

If water is going to be sprayed on a lawn either by hand or with a system, never sprinkle for only a short time. Daily light sprinkling fosters shallow rooting, fungus diseases, and the growth of crabgrass. The better way is to sprinkle (either by hand or system) for twenty minutes to an hour in each location.

SLOPES

If a large area of lawn with a long slope needs to be watered with several different lines or hand settings, the length of watering time should be shorter for the lawn at the bottom of the slope than the lawn at the top. The reason for this is that the water will continuously run downhill, causing the grass at the bottom to need less direct watering. This is important to remember because the flooded grass at the bottom of a hill is where many diseases often take hold.

FLOODING

If a lawn is being watered too much, puddles will form in depressions. This is an indication of poor drainage and shows where fungus diseases and creeping grasses can take hold. In these areas it is wise to cut back on water or to create better drainage.

REMEMBER:
- Not all dead brown spots are a result of not enough water. Many things such as chemicals, pests, and poor soil drainage can account for this.
- In climates with temperatures in the high nineties it can be necessary to water even more than once a day.
- Good watering procedures consist of regular schedules, uniform coverage, and correct timing.

SPRINKLER SYSTEMS

There is no way to create and maintain a green and beautiful lawn without ensuring that water is spread regularly and evenly. The adding of water, in the right amounts and in the right places, is essential to lawn care in all but a few climates.

WHY USE A SYSTEM OVER HAND WATERING?

Of course, the first and foremost reason is ease of use. Even manual sprinkler systems can be turned on in a moment and left to run with no worry or checkup. There are no questions as to whether the sprinkler has been placed in the most advantageous position or whether it can be moved without soaking the person in charge. And with an electrical system a person does not even have to worry about being in town to ensure that every blade and flower receive the correct and regular amount.

Other advantages are that there is better coverage in less time, increased ability to follow correct watering procedures, and savings in water bills because of more economic use. With better water procedures your ability to regulate fungus and control mold is greatly increased.

WHY AN ELECTRICAL SYSTEM OVER MANUAL?

A manual in-ground system works quite as well as an electrical one as long as the correct times and watering schedules discussed later in this chapter are adhered to. But it obviously is not as time saving and worry free as an electrical system. You have the satisfaction of knowing that the heads are covering completely, but someone must still be present to switch to each new line as the watering period is over, and someone must be there to turn the system off when every section has been covered. And unless much effort is spent to ensure accurate time and amounts, then the ability to regulate fungus and mold growth is quite lost.

SPRINKLER SYSTEM DETAILS

ELECTRICAL TIMERS

Simple electrical timers are equipped with internal workings that will rotate and set off each sprinkler line in the system once in twenty-four hours. Better timers will allow you to set the timer to only go off on certain days and not on others. Timers even better than these will provide similar features and the added ability to have certain lines go off more than once on a given twenty-four-hour cycle.

But the best timers (as most reports make out) are digital and contain the following attributes:

- Accurate A.M., P.M. clock
- Ability to program from one to three watering periods in a twenty-four-hour span
- Ability to have some lines go off twice or more a day while other lines go off only once
- Ability to set individual running times for each station without difficulty
- Easy access to manual turn-on for irregular occasions when extra running time might be required
- Battery backup in case of power failure
- Eight- to twelve-sprinkler-line capacity
- Two-week programming period

METAL PIPE VS. PVC PIPE

Certainly metal pipe is extremely difficult to break and to damage. Freezing and expanding will not turn the metal piping brittle. But PVC (polyvinyl chloride) pipe is used practically exclusively for many reasons.

Plastic pipe does not fill up with mineral growth and rust. Installation of PVC is much simpler because there is no need to thread and join ends that must be cut. Plastic pipe is easily "primered" and glued. Also, individual pieces of plastic pipe can be cut to measure in seconds with very inexpensive tools.

To make plastic pipe perform to the highest standard a few simple steps should be followed.

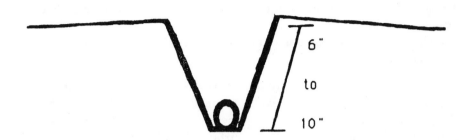

Sprinkler pipe should be buried six to ten inches deep to insure no damage from freezing or machinery.

1. Be sure that each line is buried between six and ten inches in depth. If a pipe is too close to the surface, it can be easily damaged. If it is buried too far, repairs and changes will be difficult.

2. For economical reasons, some companies or individuals may use thinner-gauge pipe throughout a sprinkler system. This is a poor idea because over time, thinner pipe (⅛″ or less) becomes brittle and can break even under normal everyday water pressure. Thinner gauge is also much more difficult—if not impossible at times—to repair.

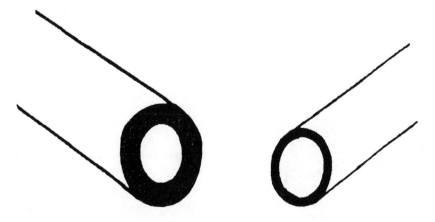

Always use thicker-gauge pipe. Thin gauge becomes brittle and is difficult to repair.

ABOUT SPRINKLER HEADS

The idea behind having a sprinkler system is to create an established pattern of spraying heads that completely and *thoroughly* covers all areas needing water.

Following are descriptions of different sprinkler heads with a brief on their characteristics.

Rainbird type. These heads are used to cover large areas because of their ability to spray long distances. School yards and parks utilize these heads. They spread water side to side at varying speeds to insure that water is flung in broken drops to the entire surface of the intended coverage area. These heads can spray straight and long, or a screw can be turned to break up the the spray in portions that are not flung as far.

Caution is advised when using rainbirds; coverage of all heads must be overlapped with each other or dry spots can occur because of uneven watering.

Straight rainbird watering. These heads spray like the above, but they move side to side more slowly, in theory to cover more evenly. They usually come in "pop up" variety. If the right brand is purchased there is an excellent adjuster to break up the spray. Still, it is important to be sure that the area of coverage for each head is overlapped.

Orbit watering heads. These heads spray in a circular pattern either in full, half, or quarter. These heads are excellent in coverage if the placement is thought out correctly. There will be a problem of clogging if for any reason dirt is allowed in the line. They also must be placed fairly high to avoid grass obstructing the field of spray.

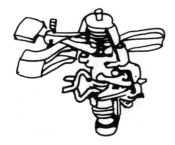

Standard rainbird-type sprinkler heads are used to cover large areas. Their spray must overlap to insure total coverage.

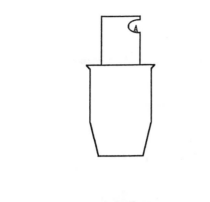

Straight rainbird heads move side-to-side much more slowly than regular rainbird heads, the purpose being to cover more evenly.

Straight rainbirds move side to side or in a complete circle.

Pop-up orbit heads. These heads are the same as the heads above except that when the water pressure is on an extender rises. These heads can be set lower in the grass to avoid being run over by a mower because the extender will rise up to the position necessary for correct coverage.

Inside of the more expensive heads, a spring is placed on the extender to bring it back into closed position. Cheaper heads rely on gravity to bring them back down, so sometimes the extensions stay elevated and are broken off by lawn mowers or passersby.

Rotary heads. These heads come in "pop up" variety and are among the top rated in the uniform spreading of water. They are equipped with springs to draw the extended portion back in after use, and the structure of the more expensive brands is quite long lasting and durable.

Each of the previously mentioned heads have different designs and variations depending on the brand, but usually the capacity of coverage is the same for each type.

ABOUT LEAKY PIPE AND DRIP SYSTEMS

Many advertisements throughout the U.S. proclaim the merits of a new and innovative technique of watering that uses less water and is much more effective at keeping a garden green and growing. These are leaky pipe systems and their derivatives.

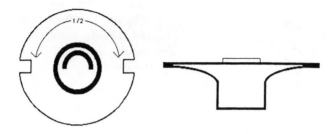

Standard orbit-type sprinkler head. These can be purchased in full, half, or quarter spray coverage.

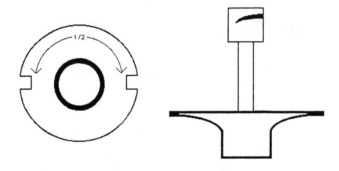

Pop-up orbit sprinkler heads can be set below the surface to keep heads from being easily damaged.

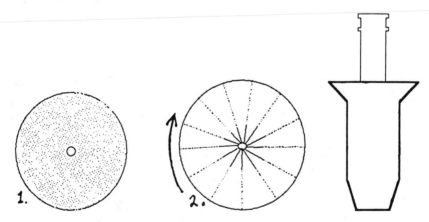

As shown in drawing 1, orbit-type heads spray in a broken pattern over their coverage area. Drawing 2 shows how a rotary head sprays broken streams. These streams rotate to soak the coverage area thoroughly.

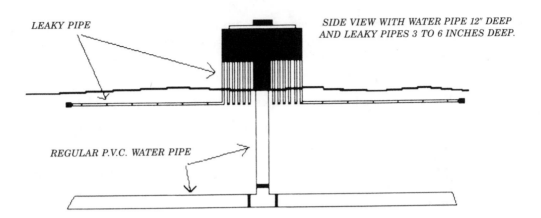

LEAKY PIPE

SIDE VIEW WITH WATER PIPE 12" DEEP AND LEAKY PIPES 3 TO 6 INCHES DEEP.

REGULAR P.V.C. WATER PIPE

This is one variety of standard leaky-pipe system. Water is transferred to roots under the soil with no water loss from evaporation. This shows a side view with water pipe 12 inches deep and leaky pipes 3 to 6 inches deep.

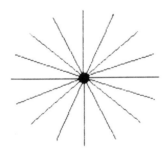

The leaky pipes are spread around the water dispenser in this star pattern.

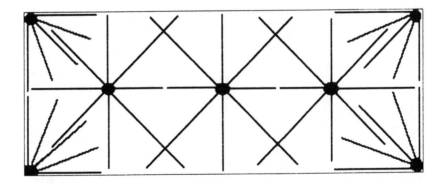

Leaky pipes are spread underground in an overlapping pattern.

These watering systems are made up of thin lines of tubing that run *under* the surface of a garden and can supply plant roots directly with needed water.

The advantages of using such a system are as follows:

- Water is applied directly to roots in a continuous arrangement.

- Fertilizer can be added to the water and distributed directly to the feeder roots without washing away or evaporating.

- Because water is fed directly to the roots without exposure to the sun or air, there is extremely little or no evaporation. This saves water and money.

In gardens around the country this procedure is an excellent way to distribute water. But in states such as Arizona, New Mexico, Florida, and Utah (to name only a few) these drip systems have not yet been perfected for the purpose of watering lawns. In these climates there is sometimes the necessity of laying tubing in every square inch of a lawn to provide the correct water coverage. This is cost and function prohibitive.

Before having one of these systems installed, check with several sprinkler outfits to ensure that a drip system is best in your area.

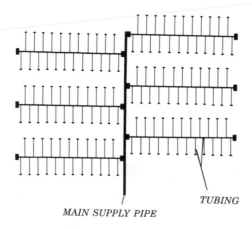

MAIN SUPPLY PIPE

TUBING

Leaky-pipe systems are also arranged flat underground in this pattern to a large area. Tiny holes allow water to drip from the entire length of tubing that is not the main supply pipe.

FIELDS OF SPRINKLER SYSTEM COVERAGE

To ensure that brown, yellow, and dead spots do not occur, the fields of spray for each head must be situated correctly to cover every square foot. Following are random illustrations that exhibit desired sprinkler head placement.

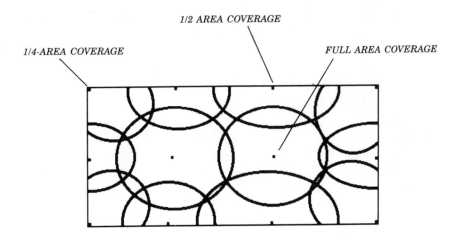

Some sprinkler head placements.

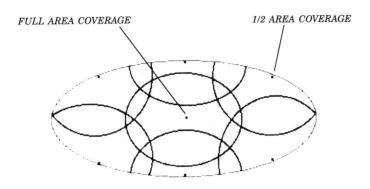

To cover an oddly shaped area it is sometimes necessary to overlap more than the area that needs to be watered.

SPRINKLER MAINTENANCE

It is virtually impossible *not* to break a sprinkler head at some point. But what must be remembered is that new heads can be replaced by *anyone* in just a few seconds, as long as pipes are not broken. If a pipe is broken, even if it is a main line, then with PVC primer and glue a repair job may actually take five minutes.

A complete sprinkler repair kit (including pipe cutters, primer, glue, broken pipe insert remover, and a few elbows and tees) will cost only about twenty-five dollars.

It is important to clean dirt out of sprinkler heads and lines at least every two years to keep them functioning at peak efficiency.

7 🌾 *Mowing*

MOWER TYPES

REEL LAWN MOWERS

Although these types were once more common than any other, today you have the best chance at sighting them in a garage, rummage, or yard sale. Most of them are of the push (manual) type, but several have been manufactured with engines.

Reel mowers cut extremely well because of their action that cuts the grass between two surfaces. The way these machines are built also helps draw the grass onto the cutting surface regardless of lawn length—something few lawn mowers do very well.

Reel mowers are not seen very often anymore for several reasons.

1. Most people prefer power mowers over manual types like the reel mower.

2. Power reel mowers are not built with a direct shaft drive, so a breakdown of chain or engine can occur frequently.

3. There are many blades to be sharpened on a reel and since the sharpen-

Simple reel lawn mower, manual style.

ing process is difficult on these types, the time involved is much greater than for other lawn mowers.

4. Because the blade is exposed, many authorities feel that these mowers are unsafe. Certainly there have been reports of objects such as small rocks being thrown directly at mower operators.

5. When blades become chipped or cracked beyond repair (a common occurrence with all lawn mowers), it is about five times more expensive to replace a reel blade.

Power-driven reel lawn mower.

SIMPLE ROTARY LAWN MOWER

Simple rotary lawn mowers are of most common use at this time, though self-propelled types are quickly catching up from behind.

Simple rotary mowers are the cheapest to manufacture and the most inexpensive to maintain. They come in different varieties, such as side baggers, rear baggers, and high vacuum baggers.

Most people prefer rear baggers because of the convenience of not having to maneuver a machine with a bag sticking far out to the side. But side baggers are excellent cutting machines in other ways. As a rule, they are considerably cheaper to buy and breakdowns are few and far between with little care and maintenance.

Rotary lawn mower with side bagger attachment.

Simple rotary rear-bagger.

High vacs are best at cutting. The way the undercarriage and grass funnels are shaped causes the grass to be sucked up (standing straight) so that it can be cut evenly, leaving an excellent appearance.

All of these but the high vacs come in gas or electric power. Though the electrics do not usually have the power of gas-run models, they are extremely quiet and light to handle. However, when an electric model breaks down, repairs are difficult and expensive.

SELF-PROPELLED ROTARY

These models, though they do not necessarily cut better than any previously mentioned, can be very convenient.

If a lawn has hills, a self-propelled mower reduces the difficulty to a third! And on a flat and even lawn, time is cut by 25 percent. The majority of people feel the job of mowing a lawn is tiring and time consuming. In a good brand, one of these models can take care of this problem.

One cautionary note: If there is a breakdown, the many more moving parts of a self-propelled mower can be very expensive and difficult to replace. A good warranty is a must!

One real advantage of these models is the feature that some exhibit of a *blade clutch*. This feature stops the blade when the handle is released, but the engine is still running. This saves wear on fingers and ignition systems. Also, on certain models this clutch will upgrade the power of a 3 horsepower engine to better than that of a 4 horsepower on a regular rear bagger. This is a wonderful feature.

POWER CLUTCH HAND BAR.

Standard self-propelled rear bagger.

A mulcher mower has a blade specifically designed to chew grass cuttings into small pieces that are left on a lawn.

MULCHER MOWER

Just recently developed to a workable and reliable standard, the mulcher mower is becoming quite popular throughout the United States. The mower has no bag and does not need one because the specially designed action of the blades chews the cut grass into small enough mulched pieces to be absorbed efficiently into the lawn. This mower will work well on just about any variety of grass, but the maintenance is a bit more difficult than that for a regular rotary mower.

COMMERCIAL EXTRAWIDE

This particular mower comes with the self-propelled feature and is extremely useful for cutting very large lawns. It is easy to maneuver even for tight turns, but of course difficult to get through small gates or garages. Blades are easy to sharpen and repairs are not usually called for very often, but most are not equipped with bags to pick up the grass.

RIDING LAWN MOWER

As a rule, riders have a large turning radius, making them impractical for any but the larger lawns. And even people with big lawns have trouble getting a rider to both front and back yards.

If a person has a private yard, fenced and enclosed, then access is usually only through a gate or garage. A rider is far too large to fit through either of these in most cases. Also, only a few of them (usually the most expensive) have bags to pick up the cut grass.

Standard riding lawn mower.

Yet when you have a large lawn, when there is available access, there can really be no substitute for a riding lawn mower. They involve so little effort. They can be adapted for many purposes, such as snow removal and garden hoeing or even equipment towing.

When a rider is indicated, do not hesitate to purchase one and save yourself time and effort.

WHICH MOWING MACHINES MAKE A LAWN LOOK GOOD?

Many people wonder about whether an inexpensive mower can make a lawn look as good as an expensive one can. The answer to this is yes, if you can make certain that a few details are present on the inexpensive machine. What really determines how well a cut lawn looks in order of importance:

- *Sharpness of the blade.* If a blade *cuts* your grass instead of tearing, bending, and bruising, then your lawn will look good.

- *Steadiness and evenness of the wheels.* If the wheels are not steady, then at different points the grass is cut short and a few inches farther away it is cut long. This effect is very noticeable on even a poor-looking lawn, let alone a healthy one.

- *Vacuum ability.* If a mower is built well to cause the grass to stand up, the cut will be even and smooth over the entire lawn surface.

- *Speed of blade.* Fast blade action causes grass to stand up, thus cutting it straighter and smoother. Faster blades also cut rather than bruise and tear.

- *Horsepower of engine.* If a lawn is thick or wet, an engine with lower horsepower will bog down and slow up. When this happens the grass will be cut poorly. Unless an engine has a power upgrading clutch, never buy a gas mower with less than 3.5 horsepower. Five horsepower is preferable.

WHICH LAWN MOWERS BREAK DOWN THE LEAST?

Over a period of time, tests have shown that lawn mowers develop several types of problems in certain areas. When purchasing a mower, make certain that these problems are corrected and eliminated.

Wheels. Too often machines are manufactured with plastic wheels that become weakened and break. All-metal wheel rims are best to surmount this problem. Poor attachment of wheels to motor housing is another *big* problem. Wheel axles hurdle this difficulty.

Handles. Maneuvering a mower around trees, gardens, and sidewalks causes strain on a mower handle, even if the mower is self-propelled. It has been noted that handles strip and break quite frequently where they attach to the mower housing. If a handle is collapsible, the metal becomes cracked and breaks directly at the joint. Look for strong, tight bolts and thick metal handles.

Bent motor shafts. If a mower has a long, thin motor shaft, the first time a hidden rock or tough sprinkler head is clipped, the shaft will bend and the mower will become absolutely useless. Buy a mower with a thick, short shaft. Most mowers are fitted with a soft metal "key" to prevent this from happening, but the blades are moving so quickly that this safety measure does not always work.

Pull ropes. These days lawn mowers are fitted by law with an engine cutoff switch at the handle to prevent injury on a moving blade. This measure, however, causes more frequent use of the pull rope. When these break, repairs are frustrating. Search for thicker and better-designed ropes.

Bag attachments. Most grass catchers are made out of metal rods and

Motor shafts that are long and skinny will break if something is struck accidentally. Look for thick shafts that are not too long.

cloth. If the cloth is thin, the grass moisture will eat through it quite soon. If the rods are too thin, they will bend under the weight of the grass and break. These bag attachments can cost a quarter as much to replace as the entire original cost of the mower. Search for a model with thick cloth, heavy rods, and plenty of support for the entire bag.

Cylinder sleeve. To manufacture engines less expensively many companies cast small engine cylinder housings in aluminum. But aluminum expands and contracts very easily and soon the piston rings cannot fill their required space to keep the oil in the engine from burning. To alleviate this problem, well-built engines are manufactured with cast-iron sleeves that do not expand as much. Ask for these cast-iron sleeves.

Cutting-height adjustment. Whether expensive or inexpensive, rider or walker, self-propelled or manual, make certain that any model purchased has a cutting-height adjustment that can be manipulated easily. *Do not* purchase a mower without this feature. Much trouble and damage to a lawn can be saved with adherence to this suggestion.

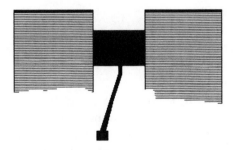

Most engine blocks are made of aluminum, which will expand and contract greatly with heat and cold.

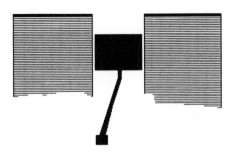

With the expansion and contraction a gap will form and oil will escape into the combustion chamber. Power is lost this way and an engine will soon break down.

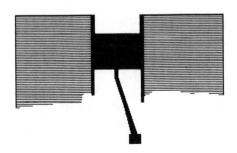

Cast-iron sleeves in a cylinder housing will contract and expand less. Such an engine will have double the life of a normal aluminum engine.

CUTTING LAWNS

Proper mowing management is an essential part of keeping a lawn healthy and green. With proper thought and planning great amounts of time and effort are saved and your lawn will thrive, remaining lush and green.

HOW HIGH SHOULD I CUT?

The first mowing in the spring should be thought of as the "cleanup" mowing. At this time the correctly determined amount of lawn should be removed to guard against the later growth of fungus diseases. A power rake (discussed in a following chapter) may be necessary.

Set your lawn mower to an inch in height, taking time to cut out and remove dead grass. Never leave the lawn mower at a one-inch setting for more than the first two or three cuttings. As the weather gets hot, the blade should be raised to anywhere from 1½ inches to 2 inches, depending on climate, variety of grass, and personal preference.

WHY HIGH CUTTING?

The height to which grass should be cut depends chiefly on the kind grown. Yet over the long period, higher cutting gives you the following benefits:

- It encourages deeper rooting.

- It reduces surface evaporation and lowers your water bill.

- It takes some of the force out of the water drops from large-volume sprinklers and thereby prevents erosion.

- It keeps roots shaded and weed seeds from sprouting.

- It is the most effective and inexpensive control of crabgrass.

HOW OFTEN SHOULD I CUT?

Frequent cutting is essential if you want to keep your lawn uniformly green. If the grass grows too tall between mowings, the green foliage will be mowed off, leaving mostly stems that are yellowed from being shaded. Grass that is mowed frequently always has sufficient foliage remaining to keep it looking freshly green and to aid the growth of deeper, more abundant roots.

Ornamental gardens are mowed as often as twice a week during the height of the growing season. But regular homeowners need cut only once a week.

Some lawns can go for as long as two weeks, but generally these do not look as good as a lawn that is cut on a more regular basis. So even if a lawn is slow growing, it is recommended that it be cut no less frequently than every ten days.

SHOULD I LEAVE THE CLIPPINGS?

This is a hard question to answer. Many case histories can be cited to prove that either leaving or removing clippings is best. So the real question is, *Do I have a particular lawn that will or will not benefit from leaving the grass clippings?*

If your lawn is deep and flexible with a good thick thatch base, it would be better to catch the clippings. If your lawn is sparse, with dirt showing in between, or even if the dirt is well covered by green grass but the thatch base is thin and you have lots of traffic, it would be beneficial to leave the clippings.

Clippings only do harm when they are left in clumps and piles. These clumps burn the grass when the sun comes out and leave yellow spots just as if a dog had left his calling card.

If you wish to let the grass clippings remain on the lawn, be sure to do this when the clippings are short so they can work down into the grass and form a light mulch. In the intermountain area, however, it is recommended that you remove the clippings and use them directly in a garden or indirectly in a compost pile, where they definitely will be more valuable.

In a low-humidity climate, grass clippings do not readily decay but rather settle around the stolons (main moisture-absorbing roots), forming an impermeable thatch that resists penetration of water and fertilizer. Also, under summer conditions of moisture and heat, matted grass clippings foster the development of fungus diseases and form a protective breeding place for sod webworms.

LAWN-MOWING PATTERNS

As a mower rolls over a lawn, its tires slightly crush and bend the blades of grass to create an unmistakable pattern of cutting. Also, since the blade is cutting one certain direction when the mower is heading forward, to turn sharply back at the end of a cut and return side by side to the last cut will create a different corridor of blade-cutting direction. This pattern can be seen in a lawn for quite some time, depending on the geographic location and density of the lawn being cut. Patterns can be arranged in some very attractive designs.

Simple Square Cut. This is done by running the lawn mower in a straight up-and-down direction one week and the next week running side to side.

Diamond Cut. Here the lawn mower is run straight back and forth at a diagonal direction for one week and at the opposite diagonal direction the next week.

Run the lawn mower straight in one direction on the first week and straight in the other direction the next week. The result will be a checkerboard.

Run a lawn mower at one angle the first week and the other angle the next week.

S-curve cut. To accomplish this, simply follow a uniform S-curve throughout the entire cutting of the lawn.

8 ❦ *Aeration*

Aeration involves putting a series of small holes in a lawn, which benefits the grass by giving the roots access to air and water. An aerator will accomplish this. One type will punch a hole in the ground of your lawn, pushing back soil to make a vacant space. Another will force a hollow shaft into the soil that will remove plugs of sod, root, and dirt. The second type is preferred by most groundskeepers because it makes the hole without compacting the surrounding soil, which defeats the purpose of aeration.

HOW AERATION HELPS A LAWN

When plugs are removed by aeration they should be left on a lawn for as long as is possible, for with each watering period the dirt clinging to a plug will wash into the ground, helping to create excellent topsoil. Lawn cutting will also reduce these plugs more quickly and easily. Plugs with clay will bake hard in the sun and require the action of continued wind, weather, watering, and mowing to break down their substance.

The holes left by aeration serve a variety of helpful purposes.

1. *Increased root growth.* In hard soil where lawn roots barely penetrate the surface, a vacuum is created that can be easily filled by new lawn roots. Increased density and depth of lawn roots means greener and more luxuriant growth. An aerator that does not remove plugs defeats this purpose. If the soil around a hole is packed harder and more densely than has the soil that has naturally occurred, lawn roots will experience an even harder time attempting to grow.

2. *Decreased water evaporation.* In areas composed mostly of hard soils or clay, water tends to remain on the surface and thus evaporate more quickly, leaving grass dry and dying. Aeration holes (usually spaced at

This is a standard aerator rod that pushes back the soil and leaves a hole. This type of rod (along with about thirty others of the same size) can be attached to a large heavy wheel, or it can be attached with three others to a piston-type assembly depending on the machine that is used.

This is a standard aerator shaft that will remove plugs of sod, roots, and soil. This can also be attached to a rolling wheel with about thirty similar shafts, or it can be attached to pistons with three others, depending on the machine used.

about 10 to 14 holes per square foot and from 1 to 3 inches deep) create a sponge effect; thousands of tiny reservoirs conserve water in the soil to keep grass green and growing.

3. *Increased watershed.* Where lawns grow on a slope and water runs off (regardless of soil makeup) these holes create a substantial and desirable watershed as each hole allows water to sink in instead of flowing off the slope. Regular aeration can save up to 30 percent of evaporation and runoff!

4. *Increased oxygen to soil.* Aeration holes allow oxygen to reach lawn roots more easily, promoting thicker and greener growth. When soil compaction is too great to allow enough oxygen below the surface or when the same compaction keeps water from draining rapidly enough, earthworms rise to the surface on a regular basis. The mounds left by these worms are most easily noted by the feel of marbles underfoot when walking on a lawn. Regular aeration causes worms to rise to the surface less frequently, leaving the lawn smooth and even.

5. *Elimination of fungus.* When water is not able to drain through the surface of a lawn (but instead pools and congeals), fungus grasses are able to gain a hold from airborne seeding. Once the seeding has taken place, the nondraining water enables the fungus to become prolific and spread. Aeration holes allow water to drain through matted lawns and tough surface dirt, removing the supportive environment.

6. *Increased fertilizer utilization.* A lawn benefits from fertilization directly to the roots. On hard soils, applied fertilizer can wash away before it reaches the roots. Aerator holes can be considered as thousands of holding bins that retain fertilizer for up to three times longer. This saves money and produces a more beautiful and valuable lawn!

WHEN IS AERATION INDICATED?

Very few lawns cannot benefit from correct and frequent aeration. Yet there are a number of signs that give specific indication of need.

HARD SOIL WITH THIN GRASS
In this instance water is evaporating, fertilizer is being washed off, and roots cannot easily spread. Free oxygen exchange is also cut off.

SENSATION OF WALKING ON MARBLES

This is caused by earthworms and indicates a lack of oxygen exchange in the soil. This symptom can also indicate difficulty in water drainage past the surface.

SLOPING GROUNDS

The difficulty here is water runoff and shallow root systems that cause lawns to be thin and dry.

LAWNS THAT ARE DRY BECAUSE OF SOIL CONTENT

With this problem an individual can continuously water a lawn and it will stay dry and dying. The soil is either too hard to allow a thorough soaking to help a lawn past the heat of the day or there are no nutrients for the roots to gain a hold on. Fertilizer is indicated to help with nutrients, with aeration to boost its absorption.

HOW OFTEN SHOULD YOU AERATE?

Some golf courses are reputed to aerate three times per year—once in the spring to help with fertilizing, in the summer to help hold water, and again during the fall to drain water past the surface and keep fungus from gaining a hold.

The average property owner does well to aerate once a year. In dry areas, many are sure to aerate twice per year.

CONTRAINDICATIONS

Don't aerate the following:

1. new lawns, planted;

2. shaded lawns that have large amounts of dirt showing;

3. grass growing sparsely, appearing only in clumps;

4. soil that is composed of light gravel and sand.

Lawns with conditions 1, 2, and 3 will only be torn up by aerator machines, negating any possible benefit. Water drains right through those with con-

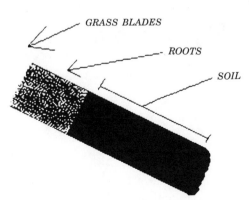

An aeration plug, shown same size, taken under excellent conditions. If the ground is hard or dry, the plug will be considerably smaller.

GRASS BLADES

ROOTS

SOIL

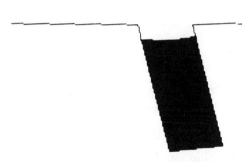

Water, fertilizer, or needed insecticides will gather inside the aeration holes and stay long enough to benefit a lawn.

dition 4, often without giving a lawn near the amount of necessary moisture. Aeration will only make this water drain faster.

REMEMBER:
You can maximize aeration by *preparing* the ground with a thorough watering.

Aeration can be done at any time during the year because of the varied and generous results. The only restriction will be if the ground is too hard because it is frozen or too dry.

9 🌾 *Power Raking*

A power rake is a machine with many free-swinging "keys" that spin at a rate of 18 to 30 revolutions per second. As these keys slam down on a lawn they force to the surface dead grass and other matter, allowing it to be picked up and hauled away.

The keys also have sharpened corners that slice into the sod for a surface aeration. Many of the advantages of aerating are produced by a power rake, but on a much smaller scale.

LAWN MOWER ATTACHMENTS

There is a power rake on the market that can be affixed to rotary lawn mowers. Purportedly this product will enable you to power rake your lawn as efficiently as a regular machine but at a fraction of the cost of either buying a regular power rake or having someone do the job for you.

The direction of movement, however, is not the same. The keys of a power rake move in a circular straight line; the mower moves in a single rotary direction and the effects upon a lawn are entirely different.

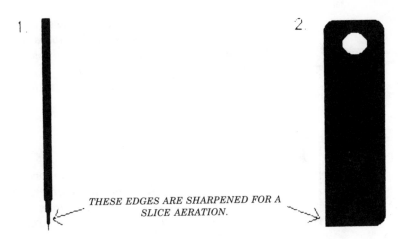

Drawing 1 is a side view of a power rake key and drawing 2 is a straight-on view. These drawings are very close to actual size and thickness.

I do not recommend using this type of mower attachment. In fact, I have seen many incidents of lawn destruction that were related to the use of this product.

BENEFITS OF POWER RAKING

Dead grass, dead leaves, and other plant matter all come together and form loam, which provides food in soil. In a lawn undecomposed grass and other plant matter are called thatch.

Grass produces thatch as a layer to protect its roots from exposure to elements such as direct sunlight, wind, and people or animals walking across it. This layer also keeps water that seeps in under it from evaporating quickly and letting a lawn dry out.

The problem is that grass does not know when to stop producing thatch, because man has mutated the different strains for his own purposes. With too much thatch a lawn can become yellow and the blades unhealthy because of lack of oxygen, water, and other nutrients that do not penetrate this thick layer.

The rotary lawn mower with a "rake" attachment moves in a flat circle, allowing grass to be torn up in the whole circumference of the circle.

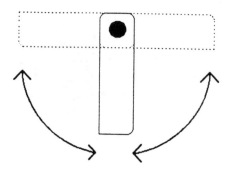

Power-rake keys can move back and forth on the retainer, which allows for give-and-take in the action. This prevents damage to the lawn.

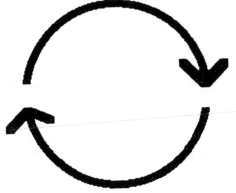

A power rake moves in the same fashion as an old-style reel lawn mower. This allows the lawn to be hit only by the keys at the very bottom of the circle.

When thatch becomes ½ to 1½ inches thick the best known way is (and always has been) to rake it out. Using a power rake is the simplest and most effective way to do this. Following is a list of the benefits of a correct power rake application.

1. *Removal of thatch.* With two thirds of the thatch removed water and fertilizer can more easily reach the roots without running off or evaporating.

2. *New lawn growth.* Lawns without choking thatch are able to send up more new shoots, thus staying renewed, young, and green.

3. *Rough surfaces leveled.* When worms rise to the surface they tend to make hundreds of lumps all over a lawn. The rapid action of power rake keys will reduce these lumps and others that may appear for various reasons by up to 60 percent.

WHEN DO YOU POWER RAKE AND HOW OFTEN?

Generally people assume that the best time to power rake a lawn is in the spring of the year. This is not always the case. Most lawns can be raked at any time during the year. There cannot, of course, be any snow, but winter is definitely no bar as long as the lawn is dry. And in many cases the *middle* of the growing season is an extremely beneficial time.

Frequency is a different matter. Unless a lawn is growing green and long with plenty of fertilizer and water during the entire growing season, it should not be power raked more than once every three years.

A competent professional should decide the necessity of power raking upon examining the lawn.

WHEN IS POWER RAKING INDICATED?

WHEN A LAWN IS YELLOW INSTEAD OF GREEN

At times the general underlying layer of grass is so thick that the dead yellow color shows more than the green, growing grass does. Removal of two-thirds of the thatch allows less of the dead yellow to show, along with leaving new space for green grass to more easily fill in.

WHEN LAWN THATCH IS TOO DEEP

When thatch is one half to an inch or more deep a lawn cannot reach peak growth, thickness, and appearance. A power rake will remove the unneeded two-thirds of the present thatch and allow peak growth to be reached.

WHEN A LAWN SURFACE IS UNEVEN

When a lawn is fairly thick with thatch and has an uneven surface, giving a person the feeling of walking on marbles, a power rake is indicated. The rapid whirling motion of the blades hitting between 18 and 30 times per second can level these lumps to quite an extent.

CONTRAINDICATIONS
Do not power rake if you have

1. thin grass growing in shade;
2. patchy lawns growing in clumps;
3. grass with less than ⅓ inch of thatch.

Lawns in these three conditions will only be torn up and damaged by the power rake and no benefit will be derived.

REMEMBER:

Dry ground = best power rake.

Power raking can be done at any time during the year if done correctly. If a rake is done during the intense heat of summer, your lawn should be watered more heavily than normal for one week to prevent burned dry spots.

10 🌾 *Fertilizers*

Fertilizer is a substance that is added to soil to help plants grow. Landscapers and homeowners spread fertilizers on lawns and golf courses to help grow *thick* green grass. Fertilizers contain nutrients that are needed for plant growth. Some fertilizers are made from organic waste, such as manure or sewage. Others are manufactured from certain minerals or from synthetic compounds produced in factories. Today, people throughout the world use billions of dollars' worth of fertilizer yearly.

WHAT IS IN FERTILIZER?

The process of *photosynthesis* (plants producing food for themselves) requires large amounts of nine chemical elements—carbon, hydrogen, oxygen, phosphorus, potassium, nitrogen, sulfur, calcium, and magnesium. It also requires smaller amounts of several other elements called micronutrients. Included are boron, copper, zinc, iron, manganese, and molybdenum. Any successful fertilizer will contain specific amounts of these elements. What determines the many differences in a brand or type of fertilizer is often simply how the mix of all these elements varies from one to another.

KINDS OF FERTILIZER

There are two types of fertilizers —*organic* and *mineral.*

MINERAL FERTILIZERS

These are the most widely used fertilizers. They supply three main elements: nitrogen, phosphorus, and potassium.

Nitrogen Fertilizers. The most widely used mineral fertilizers are produced mainly from ammonia gas. Manufacturers use ammonia in making such liquid fertilizers as anhydrous ammonia and aqua ammonia. They also use it in producing solid fertilizers, such as ammonium sulfate, ammonium nitrate, ammonium phosphate, and an organic compound called urea.

Each of these fertilizers provides the soil with large amounts of nitrogen. Some of them, including ammonium sulfate and ammonium phosphate, furnish other elements as well as nitrogen.

Phosphorus Fertilizers. Called phosphates, these are made from the mineral apatite. Finely ground apatite may be applied to soil as a solid fertilizer called *rock phosphate.* Apatite also may be treated with sulfuric acid or phosphoric acid to make liquid fertilizers called *superphosphates.*

Potassium Fertilizers. These come largely from deposits of potassium chloride. Manufacturers mine these deposits of potash or extract them with water to produce such fertilizers as potassium chloride, potassium nitrate, and potassium sulfate.

Other Mineral Fertilizers. These provide soil with various elements. Those made from gypsum, for example, supply sulfur. Manufacturers also produce fertilizers that provide specific micronutrients.

ORGANIC FERTILIZERS

Made from a variety of substances, including manure, plant matter, sewage water, and packing house wastes, these fertilizers contain a smaller percentage of nutrients than do mineral fertilizers. Therefore, they must be used in larger quantities to obtain the same results. Some organic fertilizers may also cost more, but they solve a disposal problem because organic waste has few uses other than as fertilizer. Plant matter becomes fertilizer most often in two ways—as compost or as green manure.

A Compost Pile consists of alternate layers of plant matter and soil. Fertilizer mixed with lime is also usually added. The pile is allowed to decay for several months before being used as fertilizer.

Green Manure consists of certain crops that farmers use as fertilizer. For example, some plants have bacteria in *nodules* (knotlike growths) on their roots. These bacteria take nitrogen out of the air. Such plants, called *legumes,* include alfalfa, beans, and clover.

Farmers may plant a crop of legumes and then plow the young plants into the soil. As the plants decay, nitrogen returns to and enriches the soil so it can nourish other crops.

Certain manufacturers, however, have been using these crops to produce a nontoxic organic fertilizer for homeowners to use on gardens and lawns. At this writing, these fertilizers can only be purchased at specialty stores, although their production and sale is becoming more prevalent.

FERTILIZER PRODUCTION
Fertilizer is produced in four basic forms.

1. **Straight goods fertilizer** is any chemical compound that contains one or two fertilizer elements.

2. **Bulk blend fertilizer** is a mixture of straight goods in certain proportions.

3. **Manufactured fertilizer** consists of two or more chemicals that are mixed and then formed into small grains. Each grain contains nitrogen, phosphorus, and potassium, and perhaps certain micronutrients.

4. **Liquid fertilizer** consists of one or more fertilizer materials dissolved in water. It may be sprayed on plants or soil, injected into soil, or added to irrigation water.

Most fertilizers release their plant nutrients into the soil almost immediately. Manufacturers also produce a special type of fertilizer called *slow-release fertilizer* that gives up its nutrients gradually. This type has been found useful when plants need a constant supply of nutrients over a long period of time.

FERTILIZERS WITH WEED KILLERS AND PESTICIDES
In many cases a pesticide additive in fertilizer will quickly rid a homeowner of a pest that is impossibly irritating and would linger long in the vicinity if other means were utilized. The same statement follows weed killer additives. In the case of spray fertilizers, there are few methods that can so quickly eliminate unsightly and tenacious weeds that tend to dominate a lawn or garden. But use of these additives is not without risk.

No matter what is stated by fertilizer manufacturers and companies that actively spread fertilizer over your property, high volumes of these additives are dangerous to children and animals. The more such fertilizers are put down, the longer the danger remains. People in different parts of the country have reported wildlife leaving and not returning to areas that received treatments with weed killer additives. Still other unsubstantiated reports have told of dogs getting sick and dying soon after the spraying of a formula that contains pesticides.

It is wise to regulate carefully the amount of fertilizer with pesticide and weed killer additives or to be sure to water heavily soon after an application.If you're ever in doubt, check with an authority to verify the toxicity and potency of a particular additive.

METHODS OF FERTILIZATION

There are basically three methods used for laying fertilizer down on a lawn.

1. Manually spreading a large amount (usually what is recommended on a fertilizer package) once or twice a year.

2. Having a company spray a liquid fertilizer on an average of once a month.

3. Hand spreading small amounts on a biweekly or weekly basis.

MANUALLY SPREADING A LARGE AMOUNT (DRY FERTILIZER)

This is perhaps the least effective of the three methods of fertilizing. Usually a person uses a drop spreader to disperse the amount of fertilizer that is recommended on its package. With a drop spreader an individual has little or no control over the amount of fertilizer that falls to the ground—particularly over a bumpy lawn or troublesome roots. At every bump or jolt the drop spreader can release too much fertilizer and the result is all kinds of burned spots that take months for a lawn to repair on its own, if ever.

Even if a drop spreader is not used and a large amount of fertilizer is spread on a lawn by another method, burn spots can occur. These show up weeks or even months later as thinning grass that is still green separates into clumps with bare dirt in between.

Studies have shown that with a large amount of fertilizer, much is wasted. A lawn can only use so much food in a given amount of time. The rest will either evaporate or wash away, doing your lawn no good whatsoever.

The last problem with a large amount of fertilizer spread manually is that your grass seems to suddenly grow fast and long, and it almost becomes necessary to mow twice a week for a solid month. Then, when the month is over, your lawn is back to normal (thin and no longer as green), and may seem as if no benefit was derived except to increase your exercise program. The only recognized benefit is the low cost involved, with some root growth and some lasting greening effects.

HAVING A COMPANY SPRAY FERTILIZER

The effectiveness of this method is about medium when it comes to greening and maintaining a lawn but is first rate in removing weeds. Few burns spots occur, although this depends on the reliability of the company called upon to do the job. In fact, this whole system depends on the reliability of the company dealt with, and this reliability can only be certified by reputation or time. You can always try an outfit and cancel if they do not work out.

Based on the work of a good company, the benefits are

• excellent and quick removal of weeds

• medium to good greening

• fast dispersal of fertilizer to a lawn's root system

• no effort involved

Possible problems with this system are as follows:

1. As all companies caution against children and animals playing on a lawn for the period of one to three days, there is thus a toxic risk with this method.

2. It has been reported that sometimes as much as half of the amount of fertilizer sprayed down will wash away with no benefit to the lawn. Although these reports have not been substantiated by studies and concrete results, if as much as half is washing away, a great amount of money is being thrown away.

3. In many cases a sprayed lawn will grow fast (causing a more frequent

need for mowing) for two weeks and then be back to normal until the next treatment. This is certainly not desirable.

4. These treatments for an average size lawn through a commercial company are by far the most expensive of the three methods.

HAND SPREADING SMALL AMOUNTS

This method is by far the most time- and cost-efficient procedure. A person simply figures the amount of fertilizer needed for their lawn over an average growing period. This determination can be made from experience or from information provided on packages of fertilizer. When the entire amount needed for a typical season has been calculated, divide this amount by the number of times you anticipate you will be cutting the lawn. For example, if you usually mow your lawn once a week and there are twenty-two weeks of cutting a year, divide the total amount of fertilizer by twenty-two. Apply this small amount each week after mowing the lawn by using either a push broadcast spreader or a hand-held broadcast spreader. Make sure you have used up all of the fertilizer by the time the entire lawn surface has been covered. Then water the entire applied surface.

There are many benefits to this method.

1. Because of the small amount used, no burn spots occur.
2. The cost of fertilizing is only a fraction of that of the other methods.
3. There is little or no danger of toxicity to animals or children.
4. It is root growth that determines the health, depth, and lushness of a lawn. With these regular applications the root system of a lawn feeds regularly and grows steadily and strongly.
5. Very little washes away; thus the entire benefit of the fertilizer is realized.
6. An extremely small amount of time is required.
7. Your grass is not getting so much fertilizer it grows too fast and needs to be cut more frequently than your regular mowing schedule dictates.

11 🌾 Organic Lawn Care

There is much misunderstanding about the use of the word *organic*. When it comes to using the word in relation to lawn care, misunderstanding becomes outright confusion. In aid of understanding, this chapter will cover the basic details of lawn care and then show organically related alternative procedures as they have been developed up to this time and are widely used.

Many people depend heavily on the use of chemical pesticides, herbicides, and fertilizers to keep lawns healthy. These chemicals, however, can cause damage to plants that are not being sprayed but are in the vicinity, can cause harm to passing or resident animals, and in extreme cases can cause soil and water pollution if they are overused or used improperly.

It has been postulated that where these chemicals are used by many residents, they can enter into the food or water supply and become a direct danger to people's health. For these reasons an ever increasing minority is of the opinion that lawn care methods should be more natural and organic.

FERTILIZERS

In the case of fertilizing, there are many products and procedures that can be considered organic and natural.

1. Simply cut your lawn without a bag and leave the clippings to feed the lawn. Or better yet, use an up-to-date mulching mower to grind the grass up to usable proportions for your lawn.
2. Use ground manure in light and regular amounts, since just leaving the clippings does not provide enough of the major and micro nutrients to keep a lawn at peak condition.
3. If manure is not available then use minimally processed sewage, another natural form of fertilizer. It can be quite good to use sewage, because in most cases there is no other use for the substance and there is a lot of it produced naturally on a regular basis!

Most synthetic fertilizers are made up of the exact same elements as natural fertilizers, such as manure. The only difference is that synthetic fertilizers are more concentrated. This means that you must use far more of a natural fertilizer to get the same results you achieve with the synthetic fertilizer.

Do not let the word *synthetic* fool you. Many individuals define the word as something that is unnatural and therefore undesirable. In the case of fertilizer this is not quite true. *Synthetic* just means concentrated and not produced by an organism. While potassium is extracted from plant matter naturally by the digestion of an animal, it is synthetically extracted from plant matter by a machine by a more efficient but mechanical means. However, the use you put it to is organically still the same.

It is argued that synthetic fertilizer is no longer considered organic and natural when chemical additives such as pesticides and herbicides are added to it. It is these unnatural chemicals that, when overused, have been blamed for animals being killed, plants dying, and food and water chains being contaminated. But it must be remembered that this has only been proven to be the case when very large amounts are used.

PESTICIDES

Unfortunately, the most effective pesticides are inorganic. If an organic method is desired there are not many options.

1. In cases where a certain pest is known to exist, choose and plant a cultivated variety of grass that might be resistant to or unaffected by the particular pest. This is a limited option.
2. In recent years, certain diseases, such as milky spore disease, are being studied, developed, and used that are entirely passive to a lawn but will in time totally decimate a particular pest. The above-mentioned disease, for example, attacks Japanese beetles, but can take five years to spread far enough to be effective. It could be many years before this means of ridding an average lawn of a troublesome pest is developed well enough to be of more than limited use.
3. A last method is to introduce a pest into a lawn that is passive to grass but will devour any lawn pests. Because there are always unforeseen ramifications when an outside predator is brought in to a new and unprepared ecological cycle, this method has not yet seen active commercial or home lawn use.

At this point in time, all biological methods of pest control seem to have the same negative traits. They only attack one type of pest and they take up to several years to work. This is more than likely to change at some point in time. The best way to stay apprised of any possible changes is to maintain good contact with a local nursery person.

HERBICIDES

All chemical herbicides are considered inorganic in nature. Some kill only weed seeds and others will attack only weed roots. Some chemicals only kill a weed's leafy structures, leaving the main stem to die without nourishment. But the cumulative effects on the water table and food supply are still the same. The organic methods of weed control are simple to recognize but difficult to put into practice.

1. *Pull weeds out by hand.* This takes time and effort, and only two thirds of the pulled weeds are permanently removed. The reason for this is that it is just about impossible to remove the entire root of a weed from the intertwined root system of a growing lawn. A good example of this problem is the dandelion. This weed sends down a root sometimes as deep as two feet. And if upon removal only two inches is left, the weed will return.

2. *Keep a lawn thatched and well aerated for good drainage. Institute a good fertilizing and watering program.* A healthy lawn is the best deterrent to weeds. When a lawn is thick and green, weeds cannot find a place to take root. When thatch has been kept to a minimum, weed seeds and fungus will find no place to shelter and grow.

3. *Plant cultivated varieties of grass that are resistant to weeds prominent in your location.*

4. *Maintain a good mowing schedule to keep many weeds from flourishing.* When stems and leaves are chopped on a regular basis, some weeds will die from sustained damage. Others are kept cut down to an almost unnoticeable low profile.

Unfortunately, the organic battle against weeds is an endless and ever occurring thing. Weed seeds permeate soils by the millions and they are continuously reshuffled and moved around by animals, people, and machines. But remember that even with the use of an effective herbicide, this battle will go on.

LAWN MOWING

Most methods of organically mowing a lawn are not very feasible or efficient. One such is using a grass-eating herbivore to devour the blades as they grow. Sheep will do the job, and so will horses! But they are not too meticulous about keeping the grass even, and in most urban areas there are zoning laws that would keep them out even if they did an impeccable job.

Why would someone want a method for organic lawn mowing? Because with the number of lawns created around the world and the amount of pollution contributed by the mowing machines cutting these lawns, many people are searching for a better way. Here are two plausible, reasonably ecologically sound lawn-mowing methods.

1. *Instead of using a gas-powered mower, use an electric mower.* They are quiet, they do not pollute directly and they are very efficient in terms of starting, running, and wear ratios. The only drawback is the necessity of obtaining and using an extension power cord that is long enough to reach every corner of the area to be mowed.

2. *Do not let your lawn grow fast.* It is not possible to maintain a thick and

beautifully green lawn this way, but if only a bare minimum of fertilizer is used and if the watering cycle is cut back just enough to keep the lawn a greenish-yellow and not brown, then a lawn will grow very slowly. With this method, a lawn that normally must be cut each week will only need it once every three weeks. But don't allow the lawn to dry out enough to turn brown.

As people grow more concerned about the environment and laws are passed to protect the planet from harmful substances, new methods for old procedures are developed. In one large city in California, a bill has been proposed that would require all residents in the city limits to use electric mowers. This was an attempt to do something to cut back on air pollution, but regardless of the reason, it placed disfavor on the "business as usual" approach to lawn care.

In some other states where drought has continued for three years or more, fines of up to one thousand dollars have been issued to citizens who insisted on watering their lawns in spite of emergency orders to the contrary. In many of these areas new methods of landscaping without lawns and plants that require so much watering and maintenance are being developed and used. These designs are called *xeriscapes*.

The idea behind a xeriscape is to have a landscape that requires little or no watering and little or no weeding. This would, of course, preclude all use of weed killers, pesticides, and fertilizers. But they are little comfort to those of us who still love a lawn—and they do not help with watersheds or oxygen production.

But whether this pointed disfavor grows or not, the only method of turning the environmental eye away from current methods of quality lawn care is to develop truly efficient and usable natural means of maintaining lawns. The beauty that is presented by deep green carpets of grass is too great to risk its being lost because such methods are not ecologically responsible.

12 🌱 Repairing Damaged Lawns

Whether by insect, weather, disease, or neglect lawns are often damaged right down to bare dirt. There are many means and ways of repairing depending on how the area was damaged in the first place. The following information suggests methods of repair for a broad base of general damage.

SYNTHETIC CHEMICAL AND FERTILIZER SPILLS

The grass here will turn yellow and die. There will be no sign of a root system if the soil is checked. In this case the soil will be infected for a period from three months to five years or even more depending on what has been spilled.

All soil to a depth of five inches must be removed from the dead area. Replace the soil with new high-grade dirt. Now either sod or seeds can be planted. If the replacement is done during the hot summer season, then sod is best. Be sure to match the grass variety with that of the existing lawn. If this is not done the replaced areas will be of different texture and color, which will be quite noticeable.

BARE AREAS CAUSED BY HEAVY TRAFFIC

In this instance the soil will be compacted and hard. Neither seed or sod can get a hold. If reseeding is the chosen method of replacement the bare areas must be aerated extensively. A good raking with a metal-toothed tool is required. This should be done to a depth of at least a third of an inch. A good high-traffic variety of lawn seed should be used.

If sod rather than seed will be used for replacement, the soil must be removed down to a half inch in depth in order for the soil level to remain constant with the level of unaffected areas. An extensive aeration should be performed on the areas after this soil is gone. The sod should also be of a hardy variety and it should not be rolled after placement as this will compact the soil. Regular aeration is necessary in all high-traffic areas.

DAMAGE CAUSED BY INSECTS

Be certain that the pest is eradicated. It is best to institute good fertilizing and watering procedures to strengthen pest-weakened grass. In most cases it is better to overseed than to dig up any remaining lawn and plant new sod. When overseeding it is best, if possible, to mix in a cultivated variety that is resistant to the particular pest that has damaged the lawn.

BARE SOIL LEFT BY REMOVAL OF WEED PATCHES

It is possible to use seed or sod in this situation. No real soil removal or preparation is needed other than that which is standard. A hardier grass variety might be desirable, one that will grow thick enough that weeds will be unable to gain a hold.

GRASS DEAD FROM NEGLECT

Cases have been recorded of lawns not being watered for over two years and having a complete brown and dead appearance, but after aeration and continued deep watering the grass has recovered to become strong and viable. After all, grass has been around for uncounted thousands of years longer than we have had sprinkler systems. Before spending the time and money to completely replace a lawn, be sure all avenues of watering, fertilizing, and maintenance have been explored.

WORN-OUT SOIL

Sometimes a lawn is planted in an area with extremely poor soil. Usually the soil will consist of too much gravel. Then the grass is grown for many years with few or no fertilizer applications and the cut grass blades are always bagged and thrown away. The result is a plot of grass that is thin and weak. If overseeded, none of the seeds will germinate. Fertilizer helps to green the lawn, but it gets no thicker.

In this case the only efficient alternative is to cover up the old lawn with at least five inches of grade A topsoil. Five inches is the minimum—the more the better.

Do not worry about removing any portion of the old lawn. Just be certain it is covered completely with new soil. Then a layer of fertilizer and either sod or seed can be planted.

TREES

If a tree is planted close to a lawn border and then too little water is provided, the tree will maintain feeder roots along the soil surface. The only way to avoid this is to be certain that all trees in a yard receive long and deep watering so that their feeder roots can seek well below the surface for moisture.

Once the damage has been done, however, a lawn will have veins of dead grass running like a map tracery throughout. This is because the tree depletes the grass of all available water. The only way to remedy this is to remove the tree and start over. The roots themselves must also be removed and this is often a terrible job. Some neglected homes have needed a bulldozing of the top two feet of soil to get rid of the problem wood. When the

Remove grass that girdles a tree, whenever possible. Either keep this ground bare or plant flowers. This keeps the tree trunk from being damaged, and it gets rid of the problem of unhealthy grass growing in the shade-and water deprived areas beneath a tree.

removal has been completed, new soil must be brought in and seed or sod can be used.

REMEMBER:
A lawn that is healthy and strong will be difficult to damage. And when damaged, a healthy lawn will recover quickly and easily. Maintain steady programs of watering and fertilizing to ensure less time spent in necessary lawn repairs.

13 ❦ *Lawn Care Tips from the Professionals*

Over years of working on thousands of different lawns, I've formulated a few helpful tips for the different aspects of lawn care to save time and trouble.

LAWN MOWER MAINTENANCE

1. To make a lawn mower last just about as long as you do, be certain to completely drain and change the oil at least once a year when a mower is only used for home use. If possible, change it twice a year. Professionals change the oil twice a month.
2. After every mowing, hose down the undercarriage of all mowers. Moist grass sticks to the bottom of a mower, and if it is left to dry, the protective paint coating will be eaten off. Once the coating is gone, the undercarriage will rust away.
3. Once a year, fill the mower tank with a 50-to-1 mixture of gasoline and

two-cycle oil. This will lubricate the engine and keep it running free and well. More than once a year, however, will foul up the spark plugs and valves.

4. Do not leave grass in the grass catcher. This will rot the material quite easily and quickly. Hang a catcher up to dry if possible.

LAWN CUTTING

1. To get a lawn done easily and quickly, use a good self-propelled model. These machines take the drudgery out of this dull weekly job. They seem expensive and many people think that their lawn is not enough trouble to warrant paying the extra money, but in the long run a self-propelled mower makes an owner wonder why he or she ever used anything else.

2. Keep your lawn mower blade sharp. With a sharp blade a lawn mower will cut faster and more easily. Mowers do not become bogged down with even wet grass with a good blade. Also, a lot of damage to a lawn can be avoided with a sharp blade. To sharpen a blade, remove the blade from your machine and run the edge along an electric grinder wheel.

3. Cut a lawn as long as is possible, balancing the appearance of long blades with the ability of your mower. Longer grass survives cutting easier and uses up much less water.

4. Mow a lawn only when the grass is dry. This is easier on your mower and the entire cutting will look better. Dry grass cuts with a much cleaner edge. Cutting a lawn in the morning when dew is still present is not a good idea. Quite often cutting a lawn in the late morning or early afternoon is difficult because of the intense heat that summer can bring in many areas; this leaves the late evening as the best time to mow.

5. If a gas lawn mower is being used, before cutting a lawn be sure to fill up with gas on a nongrass surface such as a garage floor or a driveway. Do this each and every time. This is necessary for two reasons. First, if a gas tank is full, a mower will continue to run better with less trouble. Second, if an individual runs out of gas in the middle of a lawn, the temptation is to run and get the gas can and bring it to the mower rather than push the heavy mower over to the gas can and then back to the cutting area. When a can is brought to a mower and used to fill a tank while the mower is sitting on a grass surface, drops will *always* spill and cause dead spots. This is a common occurrence, but it can be avoided easily. If a company is doing your lawn for you, be certain they too are filling their tanks on the driveway or road.

6. Cut a lawn without a bag wherever and whenever possible. This will help a lawn enormously in most cases and it will save wear and tear on the person doing the job!

7. Buy a pair of golf shoes and wear them when you cut the lawn. This will do a quite helpful job of aeration. Not nearly as good as an aeration machine, but helpful nevertheless.

8. Whenever a weed-trimming machine is used, the person trimming should trim in the direction that the weed eater turns. If a weed eater cuts in a clockwise motion, you should trim your lawn in a clockwise direction. This lifts the blades to be cut right into the cutting path. To trim in the opposite direction that the machine turns will bend the grass blades away and they will not be trimmed well at all. But when you are trimming a flower bed that's inside a lawn, trim counter to the spin. This will lift the blades to cut right up out of the bed and into the cutting path. Trimming in this direction will also flick the trimmed blades out into the lawn rather than onto a sidewalk or driveway, where they would have to be swept up.

9. One most important point that all professionals learn sooner or later is to follow very religiously all of the precautions posted on any machine. Here is a piece of information that hopefully will not take direct experience to teach every individual. There are enough absent toes and chopped fingers out there to teach every person in the world about where and where not to place parts of your body that you might be fond of.

FERTILIZING

1. Whenever possible, use fertilizers made from a broad range of nutrients. To use a straight mix of potassium or nitrogen or some such is only a good idea when a soil analysis has proved the lawn deficient in that specific nutrient. But since a soil analysis is not always easy to obtain, a broad-range fertilizer has a good chance of providing what is missing.

2. Always fertilize as soon as possible after aerating. When fertilizer is applied while the aeration holes are fresh and therefore still large, the fertilizer will wash into the holes and remain available for your lawn to feed off of for a longer period of time.

3. Apply small amounts of fertilizer on a regular basis rather than large amounts only once in a while. This allows a lawn a more regular and easily used source of nutrients that will keep grass green and thick.

WATERING

1. A point that is learned through years of experience in arid western climates is that most apparent ailments and dead spots of grass are from poor watering and drainage. Before any other remedies are experimented with, providing proper watering should be explored.
2. Water for long periods of time spaced farther apart rather than short periods of time once, twice, or even three times a day. This encourages deep rooting for greener lawns and better growth.
3. Do not water during the day if at all possible. Far too much moisture will evaporate as the water is falling and after the water is turned off. Watering during the evening or night allows *all* of the water to reach the soil and then sink in deeply before the evaporative light of day comes again.

MISCELLANEOUS

1. Whenever possible, remove grass completely from around any trees that are growing inside a grassy area. Create a flower bed or plant some small shrubs. This will save a tree from dying because of damage done to the trunk by lawn-mowing machines and edgers as they bump against the bark.
2. Do not attempt to grow grass under pine trees. Pine needles that drop on a lawn secrete a resinlike substance that inhibits the growth of grasses. It has also been suggested that pine tree roots also secrete this substance. With this substance present grass will not grow except in sparse amounts. If possible, cut off any branches on such a tree that are closer than six feet to the ground. Then create an attractive surface such as a flower bed or ground cover area around the tree. Ivy grows well under pine trees. Also, keep pine needles from accumulating on the lawn surface.
3. Never let leaves accumulate on a lawn in any sort of pile. If left too long, these piles will destroy a lawn the way a chemical or fertilizer spill does.
4. Overseed a lawn every other year. This allows newer and stronger cultivated varieties to be used and it keeps a lawn young and healthy-appearing. Spread seed over an existing lawn in medium quantities and then water for up to an hour in each location to settle the seeds. This process is most effective if a lawn is aerated before the seed is spread. The aeration holes provide excellent homes for new seed.

14 ❧ Lawn Care State by State

Because weather and seasons are entirely different from area to area, it is important to grow a lawn according to the natural conditions of the area in which you live. The same strain Kentucky bluegrass grown in one area by continued watering may drown in another climate with only a limited program of water applied just three times a week, because the rainfall and humidity factors are much higher in the second area than in the first.

Following is an alphabetically arranged outline for each state that will help you define what requirements must be met to maintain a beautiful lawn in your area.

ALABAMA

Much of Alabama has a 200-day or longer growing season. Central Alabama's season may last as long as 240 days. Much of southern Alabama is influenced by the Gulf of Mexico and in some areas the growing season is 265 days.

Most of the soil is a variety of loam containing sandy, stony, or silty clay. A soil additive that is often needed is lime.

In the southern areas, heavy frost can be unpredictable because of the flow of cold air into lowlands and valleys. This can have the effect of shortening the growing season.

North of Goodwater and Panda some cool season grasses like Kentucky bluegrass and tall fescue can be grown with good results. The higher the elevation the better. South of Jackson, Frisco City, and Ozark warm season grasses are mostly grown. Good varieties are centipede grass and Bermuda grass.

ALASKA

In average Alaskan soils, organic matter such as dead plants, leaves, or dead grasses should be added to create the humus that is often absent. In swampy areas it is best just to bring in new soil that will provide better drainage. Inland, out of the coastal areas, the soil is usually low on potassium, nitrogen, and phosphorus. To compensate for this problem, a broad-range fertilizer should be added before sodding or seeding. It is also often necessary to add lime.

Grass varieties that do well are Kentucky bluegrass and red fescue. Some of the cultivated varieties of Kentucky bluegrass, such as Nugget and Park, do well against the hard winter. Alaska, however, can manifest good conditions for diseases such as snow mold, so in some cases cultivated varieties of red fescue such as Aurora and Reliant might best be chosen to counteract such a problem. In areas with steep slopes it is a good idea to use a perennial ryegrass because it will grow quickly and hardily during the growing season. Some damage might occur, though, because of the hard winter.

ARIZONA

Soil in Arizona is usually alkaline. The high alkalinity interferes with the ability of grass to absorb the necessary nutrient iron. In most of the state, fertilizers containing iron are necessary. Applications of gypsum will help.

Good grasses to plant are warm season grasses such as zoysia grass and Bermuda grass. Zoysia grass can grow in shade but has a slight pest problem. It is also a strain that needs dethatching. Zoysia grass is slow to establish when seeded or sprigged. Bermuda grass is quite pest free and will look attractive. It can be planted from April to August but will look brown during the winter season.

99

ARKANSAS

In the lowlands area the soil content is fertile and drains or holds water well as needed. Drought does not often trouble this area. The soil in the upland area is often severely eroded with low fertility content. Rain is distributed evenly throughout the year with spring usually bringing a heavier amount. Lime is often a needed addition to the soil.

The best and most common grass is Bermuda grass. Many people use improved cultivated varieties of Bermuda grass for better greening or heat and shade tolerance. Areas with 50 percent shade should utilize zoysia grass. This variety does not require as much mowing but forms a thick carpet covering. In some cases centipede grass is used (though it is slow to fill in) because it forms a very attractive lawn and can survive winter well.

CALIFORNIA

The soil here is varied. Much of the state has alkaline soil and needs input of organic matter to create viable humus. In soils that contain large amounts of sodium salts, gypsum is used to create a better balance. In much of northwestern California lime has to be added to create good soil beds.

Because of the varied climates from cold to hot there are many different varieties of grass that do well in different parts of the state. Kentucky bluegrass is grown widely but has restrictions in areas such as the Imperial Valley because of disease susceptibility. These restrictions also apply to areas in Ventura and San Diego. Perennial ryegrass is used in the northern and coastal regions, where there are moderate winters. Ryegrass is popular with mixtures of Kentucky bluegrass and some of the fine fescues because it not only grows quickly but can improve disease resistance. In the areas of high heat cultivated tall fescues are used. This grass is very tolerant of heat and can look good if it is not mixed with other varieties. Bermuda grass also loves heat and can withstand long sessions without water. This grass spreads well in the summer heat and will look green and hardy if it is fertilized well and mowed high. St. Augustine grass is used sometimes in California in areas with warm seasons but high shade. It only does well in these shade areas.

COLORADO

Most of the soil in this state is alkaline without very much iron content. Iron-containing fertilizers must be mixed well with soils to grow thick grass. Some of the mountain areas are dry for much of the year and the good-grade soil is shallow. To keep a lawn growing, regular fertilizer applications are needed.

The most commonly used grass is Kentucky bluegrass, but because of a problem with leaf spot it is better to use a cultivated variety such as Baron, Columbia, Midnight, or Sydsport, or even a blend of all four.

Thatch is common in many of the lawns because of the climate but power raking will take care of this. One of the main causes of lawn problems in this state is inadequate watering. For best results a well-planned and regular watering program is essential.

CONNECTICUT, MAINE, MASSACHUSETTS, NEW HAMPSHIRE, RHODE ISLAND, VERMONT

All of these states can be considered as a specific region having many similar characteristics. Both the soil and climate are relatively mild throughout these states. There is a high amount of rainfall but the soil is usually fairly shallow and not good at utilizing water. With this inability to properly hold moisture, summer watering is essential. Adopt a good watering program for best results. New soil is usually helpful. Lime is almost always a strong requirement.

The most widely grown grass is Kentucky bluegrass with sometimes a mixture of the fine fescues or perennial ryegrass.

DELAWARE, MARYLAND, KENTUCKY, NEW JERSEY, WEST VIRGINIA

These states are mentioned here together because of the similarities they all embrace. The Appalachian Mountains and West Virginia have cool summers. Washington, D.C., and Maryland have hot summers. But throughout all the rainfall is adequate and frequent. Many of the soils will be found to be adequate for ready planting. Others will be high in acid content and still others will be high in alkalines. Lime and gypsum are commonly used for these ailments. Soil testing for accuracy in determining your soil content is a necessity.

Mixture of Kentucky bluegrass, fine fescues, and perennial ryegrass are most useful in the cool summer areas. In hot summer areas it is best to use the tall fescues. A highly rated cultivated variety to use in these areas is Kentucky 31. Bermuda grass is used once in a while in New Jersey, Maryland, and Delaware.

FLORIDA

This state has a climate that is dominated by the ocean waters on three sides. There are several different soils. Along the coast there are marshes and sandy areas. Inland there are more fertile soils, especially those reclaimed from the swamps. Lime is often used.

There are many grasses that grow well in Florida—Bahia grass, Bermuda grass, centipede grass, St. Augustine grass, and zoysia grass. Bahia grass is better adapted to central Florida. Bermuda grass is used to make very attractive lawns in many areas. But centipede grass makes a good low-maintenance lawn in almost all areas (lowland or highland). St. Augustine grass, though mostly used in the shady areas, is the most popular grass in the state. But good watering, disease, and insect-control programs are essential to keep looking good. Overseeding all of these previously mentioned varieties is often done with perennial ryegrass and bent grass.

GEORGIA

More than half of the state has a sandy soil, while the rest is mostly piedmont that is clay and clay loam. Almost all of the soil has a high acid content, but with lime and organic plant matter added it is capable of good growth with the grasses mentioned below.

The most popular grass is Bermuda grass, along with the cultivated varieties of Tifgreen, Tifdwarf, and Tiflawn. Where the soils are wet, however, a variety of grass called carpet grass is used. Centipede grass is used in wet soil but can be slow to start. For shade areas St. Augustine grass is used. In the mountains tall fescues are the most planted.

HAWAII

Most soil in this state is sandy or volcanic and not very acceptable for lawn grasses to grow. To make an improvement it is necessary to add organic plant matter such as dead grass, manure, leaves, and compost.

A common variety of planted grass is Bermuda grass. It is hardy and can take a beating in the form of heavy traffic. Another grass that is used is Emerald zoysia grass. This variety is slow to establish but will become extremely thick in several years. St. Augustine grass is planted in Hawaii, but it is often called by other names. It will grow quite well in shaded areas.

IDAHO

This soil is mostly of a clay content. Some areas contain rocks that must be removed before planting can be done. It is best to make sure that as much organic material is worked into the soil as is possible.

Kentucky bluegrass is used most of the time but is often mixed with the fine fescues to give it shade tolerance. If the cold of winter does not reach a certain area, perennial ryegrass is sometimes used. In areas that are not watered on an artificial basis, the native American varieties of buffalo grass, blue grama, and wheatgrass can be used. These are strictly for nonornamental coverage and require low maintenance.

There are many reported cases of powdery mildew and snow molds in Idaho, so a grass resistant to these diseases is preferable.

ILLINOIS

This state has three distinct climatic regions. The upper region (northern) has the coldest and longest winters with warm summers; the middle section of the state has cold to moderate winters with warm summers; and the southern section has mild winters with hot and humid summers. Over 65 percent of the state is prairie with a soil that is dark brown, deep, and fertile. In fact, most prairie soil was made and developed by long years of growing grass. Lime is often needed in the soil.

Kentucky bluegrass is the best and most often used grass, especially if a mix of red fescue or ryegrass is used as well.

INDIANA

Half of this state is prairie with the typical deep fertile soil that permeates prairie regions. The southern portion of the state has many hills, and though the soil is still quite fertile, it is shallower in many places. About 30 percent of the areas in the state will need lime added.

As in many other states, Kentucky bluegrass is the most popular grass variety except for some areas in the south. It can be good in most areas to plant a mix of bluegrass with some of the fine fescues and ryegrass. For the southern areas it is best to plant varieties of Bermuda grass or zoysia grass.

IOWA

The climate in this state can be quite hot in the summer with hot, dry winds that can damage lawns that are not watered every day. The soil is fertile but often lacking lime.

Though Kentucky bluegrass and some of its cultivated varieties are used most frequently, tall fescues make tougher lawns for high traffic.

KANSAS

In the northwestern portion of this state the soil is acidic. The same is true for the southeastern portion. In western Kansas, where the great plains stretch out for vast distances, the soil is often windblown and erosion is a great problem. Hardy grasses are needed to hold the soil and its fertility factors in place.

Zoysia grass and Bermuda grass are used quite frequently throughout the state, but it is often more feasible to use the natural grasses, such as buffalo grass or blue grama. These natural grasses can be maintained on only the natural rainfall if necessary.

LOUISIANA

The greatest part of Louisiana is made up of level land with sandy but fertile soil. Much of the soil is acidic and regular applications of lime are necessary.

Centipede grass is the most popular grass variety because it will grow just about anywhere in the lower south, even in poor soil. But Bermuda grass will grow quite well in soils with moderate fertility. Sometimes St. Augustine grass is used for a well-kept and fertile area.

MICHIGAN

Most soil in Michigan is highly acidic, but lime is not always directly applied because the water often contains enough of the nutrient. Much of the soil is low in fertility, but if organic matter and regular fertilizer are added, the soil will produce a beautiful lawn.

The most widely grown grasses are cultivated varieties of Kentucky bluegrass and the fine fescues. These cultivars are Adelphi, Baron, Midnight, and Sydsport (Kentucky bluegrass cultivated varieties) and Aurora, Reliant, and Shadow (fine fescue cultivated varieties).

MINNESOTA

Soils in this state range from sandy to sandy loam and all the way on to heavy clay. Add plant matter to these soils to increase fertility. Lime is not added more than once every five years or more.

Popular grasses are mixtures of Kentucky bluegrass and red fescue. Perennial ryegrass is also popular in many areas, but usually it is best to plant a cultivated variety that is resistant to severe winters.

MISSISSIPPI

Both the plains area and the river delta areas of this state are quite fertile. There are usually high levels of acid in tested soils. Lime should be added on a regular basis in about 70 percent of the state.

Bermuda grass is the most popular grass choice. Zoysia grass, though it is slow to grow, is planted in some areas because it is a more attractive and finer lawn. St. Augustine grass can be planted in the shady areas but will have only low winter tolerance.

MISSOURI

Much of this state is either lowland and slightly hilly or prairie. The soils in all areas are quite fertile, but the prairie areas are dryer of rainfall and humidity. Most areas are also quite acidic and lime must be added.

There are many varieties of grass that do well in this state, including Kentucky bluegrass, fine and tall fescues, and perennial ryegrass. Improved cultivated varieties of these strains work well also. Zoysia grass is used in a few areas where there is high heat and a long growing season.

MONTANA, WYOMING

These two states have much the same conditions. The soil in both states usually lacks fertility and a large amount of organic plant matter must be added to improve a growing area. Alkaline is usually found instead of acid.

Kentucky bluegrass is the most popular grass but is even better if mixtures of fine fescues are also added. Fine fescues alone will form shade-resistant and drought-resistant lawns. Perennial ryegrass can be used, but it is low in winter tolerance and these states are quite cold at times. In cases where supplemental water cannot be added, the native American continental grasses such as buffalo grass and blue grama grass are sometimes used, though not for ornamental purposes.

NEBRASKA

Soil in this state is usually sandy or sandy loam. Often the soil is shallow and needs improvement with organic matter. Lime is not generally added at any time. The winters are mild compared to other states but the summers are semiarid. Good watering programs are absolutely necessary.

Mixtures of Kentucky bluegrass and fine fescues are the most popular lawns. Perennial ryegrass is used in areas with the mildest winters. Tall fescues are used for hardy lawns in the dry areas but winter tolerance is not very good.

NEVADA

This state has high alkaline content and is low in fertility. Organic matter must be added to remedy this problem. Water is a problem throughout much of the state and summer dryness is the most common lawn problem.

Kentucky bluegrass with a fine fescue mixture is the usual lawn that is planted. Tall fescues are planted in mixtures in some areas but is planted alone for best appearance. In the southern dry areas, Bermuda grass is used almost exclusively for the finer lawns. Some Bermuda cultivated varieties are used for home ornamental gardens but high maintenance is required.

NEW MEXICO

The soil here is usually alkaline and low in fertility. Added organic matter is necessary. To wash salts from the soil it is sometimes beneficial to flood a lawn area. Applications of gypsum will help also.

Bermuda grass is an excellent grass for most locations where the heat is high and water may be available only in limited quantities. In areas where the weather might be cooler, Kentucky bluegrass is found. It is important to cut this grass as high as possible to help with heat resistance. In these same areas where the weather is cooler it is also possible to plant tall fescue blends.

NEW YORK

The climate in New York is mostly temperate with medium to high humidity. Summers can be hot and dry for short or long periods, so good watering programs are essential. Most of the soil is fertile and needs no organic plant matter added, but on occasion it is necessary to add lime.

Kentucky bluegrass mixtures are grown the most frequently. Red fescue is often mixed with the bluegrass to counteract the dry season problems. In the warmer areas of the state it is possible to plant zoysia grass for a beautiful-appearing lawn. Some improved cultivated varieties of all these previously mentioned grasses will be more heat-, disease-, and pest-resistant for the New York region.

NORTH CAROLINA

This state can be divided up into three regions: The Blue Ridge Mountains, the Coastal Plain, and the Piedmont. The soil is fertile in almost all areas but can be shallow in the mountains and Piedmont. The soil is quite acidic. Lime is always necessary.

In the western and mountain portions of the state the best grass to use is Kentucky bluegrass. In the lower elevations and flatter areas it is better to use Bermuda grass, tall fescues, or zoysia grass. In the warmer sections it is possible to use centipede grass or even St. Augustine grass if the area is close to the coast.

NORTH DAKOTA, SOUTH DAKOTA

These two states are closely related in most conditions. In the eastern regions of the states can be found fertile, loamy soil. In the west the soil will range from extremely poor to excellent. In both the east and the west the fertile portions can be quite shallow and new soil must be brought in.

Most lawns are made up of mixtures of Kentucky bluegrass and fine fescues. If water applications are not available, the native American grasses such as buffalo grass and blue grama are able to withstand a hard and dry climate.

OHIO

The best soil in this state is in the northwestern portion that is relatively flat and even. The southeast portion of the state is mostly fertile, but because of the many hills this fertile soil is mostly shallow. In a few areas such as the north-central portions, the soil is often poor and stony. Soil will need to be brought in to grow grass in these sections.

The best grass for this area is undoubtedly Kentucky bluegrass. Some of the cultivated varieties such as Adelphi, Fylking, and Sydsport are even better adaptations for the state. In places of high shade some fine fescues can be used, but are grown best as mixtures with Kentucky bluegrass.

OKLAHOMA

The western sections of this state are cool, dry, and flat, while the eastern portions are cool and moist with much more rain than the west. Soil in the east is above average in fertility, while the west is only average in fertility. Both areas are good to excellent for growing grass. Lime is often a requirement.

The most popular grass is Bermuda grass. A few cultivated varieties of Bermuda grass will do well also. In areas where supplemental water is not available or where ornamentation is not a factor, a native American grass such as buffalo grass will do well.

OREGON

In almost all of Oregon the soil is fertile with a lot of humus for good plant growth. On the west side of the cascade range the weather is mild, rainy, and humid. On the eastern side of the cascade range the weather is colder and less humid, and the area receives much less rain.

Many different grasses will grow in Oregon. Included are Kentucky bluegrass, perennial ryegrass, fine fescues, and sometimes creeping bent grass. In the western areas, improved perennial ryegrass is preferred, but it must be planted only where the winters are not severe. Cultivated varieties that are resistant to rust and red thread are good to plant in most areas of the state.

PENNSYLVANIA

The soils along most of the Allegheny Plateau are often stony and thin. The soils in areas similar to the Scranton area are mostly tough clay. In both areas a lawn will benefit from large amounts of organic matter added to the soil before the lawn is installed. Regular fertilizer is needed in all areas and in most applications of lime are necessary.

Kentucky bluegrass is most often used. Some bluegrass cultivated varieties are Adelphi, Columbia, Glade, Midnight, and Victa. Where there are cooler areas, red fescue is sometimes used. This is the case most often where there is a lot of shade to contend with.

SOUTH CAROLINA

The climate in South Carolina is warmer than the climate in North Carolina. The soil of the Piedmont is relatively fertile but can be shallow in places. New additions of good soil can remedy this. The soil of the coastal plains is fertile and deep in most areas and will grow grass quite well. Most of the soil will be found to be acidic and applications of lime will be necessary.

Where there are sandy hills or along most of the coastal plain it is best to use Bahia grass. Bermuda grass is also used extensively and can be grown well in many areas. In the Piedmont areas, centipede grass is very useful and popular. On occasion zoysia grass is used, but only where the heat is not too severe.

TENNESSEE

In the eastern portion of the state there are many mountains that shelter broad fertile valleys. Though the soil in these regions is made up of sandstone, shale, and limestone, it is quite fertile and productive. There is a second area in Tennessee called the Central Basin. This area is surrounded by some ridges called the Highland Rim. This basin has fertile limestone soil and is most excellent for growing grasses.

Kentucky bluegrass is the most widely used variety of grass. In many ares the use of zoysia grass and the tall fescue is increasing. In areas of frequent drought it can be better to use Bermuda grass because of its ability to go without water for longer periods than other grass varieties.

TEXAS

Because of the size of the state there are many varied climates. In some areas in the east the rainfall is almost as high as anywhere in the country, and in some places in the west the rainfall is almost as scarce as in most deserts. Most of the soil in the whole state, however, is lacking in fertility and humus. Adding large amounts of organic matter can be extremely helpful for long-term lawn growth. Good fertilizer programs are necessary in most of the western portions of the state and lime can be needed in all areas.

The most often grown grasses are Bermuda grass and St. Augustine grass. Bermuda grass is the easiest to plant and care for while St. Augustine is better at pest and disease resistance and can in certain areas be attractive in appearance. A cultivated variety of zoysia grass called Emerald is used in some southern portions of the state because of how thick and green it can grow. But it will have little if any cold tolerance. In areas where water supplements cannot be used, buffalo grass will grow with only the natural rainfall, though it can be difficult to get it started.

UTAH

Almost all of the soil in Utah is low in humus and organic matter. Additions of plant matter are of considerable help before a lawn is planted. Most of the soil in the state is sandy and gravelly. In other portions there is hard-packed clay. In much of Utah there are high concentrations of alkali. Gypsum added to the soil will cure this problem. Another problem that will occur frequently is yellowing due to lack of nitrogen and lack of iron. Nitrogen and ferrous fertilizers are a must. Summer drying is perhaps the worst cause of lawn problems. In most areas sprinklers must be used every day.

Kentucky bluegrass is the most popular grass grown, but it does better when cut to the longer lengths. Any cultivated varieties that are resistant to high heat and dry air are more successful. For shaded areas, mixtures of fine fescues with Kentucky bluegrass should be used. Perennial ryegrass can be used for a quick-growing seeded lawn, but Utah winters are so harsh that only improved cultivated varieties such as Manhattan II are very successful. In the extreme southern portion of the state near the city of St. George some of the warm-season grasses such as Bermuda grass will do well.

VIRGINIA

Some soil in Virginia will be found to be acidic and others will be alkaline. A soil analysis will confirm the pH and either lime or gypsum can be added to counteract these problems. With care, most areas in this state will produce good lawns.

Tall fescue is planted most extensively in this state because it is a hardy strain. But other grasses can work well in the right areas. On the west side of the Blue Ridge Mountains and in many northern areas Kentucky bluegrass, perennial ryegrass, or fine fescues should be planted. East of the Blue Ridge Mountains and in the southern areas Bermuda grass and zoysia grass should be planted. Cultivated varieties of Bermuda grass that grow well in the southern areas are Tufcote and Midiron.

WASHINGTON

Soils in this state are low in humus and plant matter. Any planted lawn will be helped by adding leaves, dead plants, and cut grasses. Because of the acidity of the soil lime will need to be added in most areas.

The best grasses to plant in the eastern regions of the state are mixtures of Kentucky bluegrass and fine fescues. In the western regions, perennial ryegrass will make a quick-growing and fine lawn. In the cooler and shaded areas of the western regions, bent grass is often grown for an attractive lawn.

WISCONSIN

The winters in this state are very cold and harsh. Most of the soil throughout the state is acidic from the evergreen forest that covered the state for hundreds of years. But if treated with lime and some fertilizers, the soil can be dark and rich and will produce excellent lawns.

The best way to create a hardy lawn that will survive the hard winters is to plant a blend of three or more Kentucky bluegrass cultivated varieties. In dry, sandy, and shaded soils the use of fine fescues is suggested to produce an attractive lawn.

15 🌾 Lawn Care Calendar

The factor that is most important to the timing of your lawn care details is the average mean temperature of the area that you live in. The growth of a lawn is determined by many different components such as soil makeup, nutrient availability, and water, but the most prominent factor in lawn growth is heat.

Following is a broad-range lawn care calendar that divides the United States into three regions. These regions are determined not by placement on any map but by average yearly temperature, soil variations, and growing season length. It is important to keep in mind that conditions and timetables may vary somewhat in your particular area.

To use the calendar, simply examine each region until your state is found. After your region has been determined, follow the calendar suggestions as the physical conditions current in your area allow.

SOUTH ZONE

TEXAS	MISSISSIPPI	NORTH CAROLINA
OKLAHOMA	LOUISIANA	FLORIDA
ARKANSAS	ALABAMA	VIRGINIA
TENNESSEE	SOUTH CAROLINA	GEORGIA

NORTH ZONE

NORTH DAKOTA	MARYLAND	CONNECTICUT
SOUTH DAKOTA	DELAWARE	MASSACHUSETTS
NEBRASKA	INDIANA	VERMONT
KANSAS	WISCONSIN	NEW HAMPSHIRE
MISSOURI	IOWA	MAINE
ILLINOIS	MINNESOTA	PENNSYLVANIA
KENTUCKY	NEW JERSEY	OHIO
WEST VIRGINIA	NEW YORK	MICHIGAN
	RHODE ISLAND	

WEST ZONE

ALASKA	ARIZONA	OREGON
HAWAII	NEW MEXICO	WASHINGTON
UTAH	WYOMING	COLORADO
CALIFORNIA	MONTANA	
NEVADA	IDAHO	

NORTH ZONE

JANUARY TO FEBRUARY

This is the time to treat any diseases that have occurred in previous years, such as snow mold or gray mold. Do this during a winter thaw. Also apply preemergence weed controls at this time.

MARCH TO APRIL

This is a perfect time for planting either seed or sod. It is best to wait until the temperature reaches a steady 65 degrees Fahrenheit for laying sod, but it can still be placed anytime during the entire growing season. Seed can be laid down during any thaw. The best growing time for seed is during the spring or during the fall when the temperature is between 65 and 80 degrees. This period is ideal for applications of either gypsum, lime, or straight fertilizers.

Spring is a prime time for power raking. A lawn will recover quickly in an average temperature of 70 degrees with plenty of natural moisture falling. Removing thatch will also help a lawn get better use out of a preemergence herbicide or fungicide.

This is a good time to aerate. Aeration will open up the soil to allow air, fertilizer, herbicides, fungicides, and even water to penetrate more thoroughly and deeply.

During these months, weeds such as crabgrass and dandelions will begin to sprout. Before the temperature reaches a five-day stretch of 65 degrees or more, there is still time to place some preemergence controls. If the weeds are already growing, now is the best time to apply postemergence controls, before the weather gets too hot (85 degrees or more).

MAY

If heavy rains have fallen for a while and you utilize a program of heavy fertilizing once or twice a year, it is now time to fertilize. If you have Bermuda grass or zoysia grass, it will be coming out of the dormant brown phase at this time. Fertilizer will speed up the greening process.

This is good weather for sprigging and plugging or sodding, especially in areas where Bermuda grass and zoysia grass are being planted.

This is a good time to overseed and add a grass mixture to your lawn that might make up for what your lawn is lacking—quick greening or disease resistance.

JUNE

Fertilize any Bermuda grass or zoysia grass throughout the growing season. If you have adopted a weekly fertilizing program, apply necessary amounts each week after mowing.

If preemergence controls were not used for weeds, many will be growing at this time. It will be too hot to use many herbicides at this time. A temperature of 85 degrees Fahrenheit is the outside limit within which most chemicals can be successfully used. Carefully read all labels to be certain of correct usage.

During this month many insects will make their presence known. Brown dry patches will appear, and when the grass is lightly pulled on, it will come easily from the ground or will roll back like carpet. Some insects will be observed at their work; others will need to be searched for by lifting a section of sod. Use appropriate chemical controls.

JULY TO AUGUST

Cool season grasses will go dormant in the hot weather of these two months. Growing is slowed and greening becomes a problem. Continue watering and fertilizing programs for best results.

Warm season grasses such as Bermuda grass are growing fast at this time and will need nutrients (in the form of fertilizer) added in regular amounts.

August is a good time to prepare an area for a new lawn. You can take the time to add fertilizers and new soils and perform all of the necessary grading or leveling before the cooler growing season arrives.

This is the time when many adult beetles lay their eggs in the lawn. When they quickly hatch, tiny white grubs will appear and feed on the grass blades. When cool weather arrives these grubs will disappear down a depth of two feet or more to survive the winter. It is better to catch them now in the warm weather. Use appropriate chemical controls for best results.

Summer is also an excellent time for aeration. The holes provide better drainage for soils that are baked hard by the sun and allow fertilizers and oxygen to work more efficiently.

SEPTEMBER

After the summer has passed, warm season grasses are still lush and green and cool season grasses are reviving with new life.

As the weather cools down below 80 degrees Fahrenheit it is possible once again to use herbicides to control weeds. Most of the broad-leaved weeds can be controlled this way.

This time is the best time of the entire year for planting. The warm days and cool nights will encourage sods, sprigs, and seeds to grow fast and thick.

Power raking is done extensively on established lawns during this time because grasses are able to recover more easily without the extremes in heat that summer brings.

Aerating is good to have done at this time. The newly created holes will provide drainage for fall and winter moisture that can cause diseases and spores to grow.

September is also an excellent time to overseed both warm season grasses and cool season grasses. The seeds will grow well and fast.

OCTOBER TO NOVEMBER

For at least the first week and a half of October it is still possible to fertilize and plant. Fertilizer and seeds that are not used or sprouted before snow flies will carry over to the next year.

If snow mold was a problem during the spring, the disease organisms will still be present. Late October or early November is the best time to use the correct chemical to rid your grass of this problem.

Aeration for good drainage of fall and winter moisture is still recommended before the snow falls.

SOUTH ZONE

JANUARY TO FEBRUARY

In the South, many areas will warm up quickly and preemergence controls will definitely need to be applied during one of these months.

In the warmest areas of the South, where some lawns stay green all year round, warm season grasses such as St. Augustine grass, Bahia grass, and Bermuda grass will benefit from an early application of fertilizer. This will make the dormant brown season shorter.

In states that are mild for most of the year it will be warm enough to bring grubs to the surface to feed on the grass. While at the surface, these grubs are vulnerable to chemical control.

MARCH TO APRIL

When the temperature of 70 degrees Fahrenheit is reached and sustained for more than five days, the growing season has officially started. Warm season grasses will begin to show new life through the dormant brown.

Fertilizer should be applied to several varieties of warm season grasses during March. Bermuda grass and St. Augustine grass are two examples. During April, carpet grass, centipede grass, and the cool season grasses should be fertilized.

It is good to set the mower low for the first cut in either March or April. This will clean out some old dead growth and allow warmth and sunlight to stimulate warm season grasses.

Although sodding can be done anytime during the warming season, these two months are an excellent time to get a new lawn laid down. The warm days and cool nights before summer will encourage excellent growth.

Before the temperature reaches a steady 65 degrees or higher it is still time to use a preemergence control for weeds. Check labels to be certain of correct use. If the temperature is higher than 65 degrees but still lower than 85 degrees, it will be an excellent time to use postemergence controls. Postemergence controls work best just as the plants are sprouting.

In states where the spring weather is cool and moist for long periods, fungus disease will grow and develop. Leaf spot and cottony blight are two examples. Appropriate chemical control is called for in these cases.

MAY

May is an almost perfect month for planting grass in the South. Warm season grasses can be planted later, but they might not have time to establish themselves before cool weather and the dormant season arrives.

It is important to fertilize all warm season grasses this month except carpet grass and centipede grass. If yellowing persists, fertilizers with iron may be needed. Any warm season grasses will need nitrogen also. This is a good month to apply either lime or gypsum according to which is needed.

Power raking is needed for lawns that have accumulated one half inch or more of thatch. This is especially true of Bermuda grass and St. Augustine grass.

Certain weeds will be in bloom at this time; dandelions are one example. Yet while spurge, oxalis, and others will not be blooming, they will be just as troublesome. Before the temperature reaches 85 degrees Fahrenheit or higher it is important to use the chemical herbicides that are prescribed for the weeds of your particular lawn.

Aeration will (as always) be of great help in maintaining your lawn before the hot weather arrives. Aeration will increase the water supply to the root system, allow fertilizer to reach feeder roots, and will allow needed air to circulate around the entire plant.

JUNE

Cool season grasses will start to yellow and slow down as the weather gets hotter. Good watering will help with brown spots. Warm season grasses should be looking toward perfection. But as with the cool season grasses, water is a main ingredient in keeping a lawn green as high heat sets in.

Weeds that have not been taken care of will really show during this month and the next. As lawns are weakened from the heat, weeds are able to gain a better hold. Many of these weeds will need to be removed by hand, since the weather is too hot for most herbicides to be safely applied.

Both Bermuda grass and zoysia grass will require fertilizer in this month, since they will be growing profusely. Fertilizer need only be applied to cool season lawns that are on a weekly small-amount program.

Sod webworms will become a problem this month. They can first be identified by the moths hovering around a lawn at dusk to lay their eggs. When the eggs have hatched they will feed on grass blades at night and burrow in the roots during the day. Both cinch bugs and armyworms will appear at this time. Both of these pests can be seen during the daylight hours, though cinch bugs may require close examination for discovery.

JULY TO AUGUST

During these hot months, water will be required in large amounts by all lawns. It is important to remember that deep watering will train a lawn to be green and flourish even during these high temperatures.

It is important to raise the cutting height of your mower for these two months to provide shade and evaporation protection. This will also keep a cool season grass from going dormant in the heat.

Keep fertilizing as needed to fill your specific program. Both Bermuda grass and zoysia grass will need applications.

If the weather in your area is hot, rainy, and humid, watch for diseases such as brown spot and gray leaf spot on St. Augustine grass.

SEPTEMBER

This month is the best time of the year for planting any cool season grasses. The warm days and cool nights will accelerate growth to the maximum amount.

As the weather cools down below the 85 degrees Fahrenheit mark, it is possible to use many postemergence controls that have survived the spring campaign against them. It is also a good time to place down some preemergence controls for certain annual grasses.

At this time it is important to maintain a perfect fertilizing schedule. For the warm season grasses it is the last fertilizing of the year (except in the far South and when certain programs are in use) and will provide good growth in these fall days. For the cool season grasses, this is the time when fertilizer is stored in the plant system to help with winter survival. The better the fertilizer storage, the better the winter survival.

OCTOBER TO NOVEMBER

In the deep South there is still time to plant in October. Both months, however, are good for overseeding the warm season grasses with cool season grasses that will remain green and will hide the dormant brown color of the warm season grass.

The weather is perfect in most of the South for getting rid of broad-leaved weeds with chemical sprays. Many of these weeds are more easily attacked during this time of the year.

In the deep South it is time for the one last fertilizing that will build up strength in warm and cool season grasses for the winter months.

WEST ZONE

JANUARY TO FEBRUARY

In areas of southern California and Arizona it is time to plant and fertilize. The mean temperature should be a sustained 65 degrees Fahrenheit.

In all areas it is time to get rid of crabgrass before it starts by using preemergence controls. It is necessary to have clear, dry weather in places such as Oregon, California, or Arizona before applying, and it is necessary to wait for a thaw before applying in places such as Utah, Idaho, or Colorado.

MARCH TO APRIL

Now is one of the best times to plant all of the cool season lawns. If sod, seed, or sprigs are planted, grass will have time to establish itself and gain somewhat of a root system before hot weather arrives.

In the southern areas of California and Arizona the cool season grasses will be growing well at this time. In the other states the green will be beginning to show and the grass will get thicker. Warm season grasses will begin to come out of the brown dormant phase. Correct and regular applications of fertilizer will speed up the awakening process of both warm and cool season grasses. This month is also an excellent time for laying down gypsum or lime where needed.

Aerating before fertilizing will help a lawn absorb the nutrients much more efficiently and without waste. Aeration will also allow water and air to revive winter dormant grasses.

This month is a good time to power rake lawns that have over a half inch of thatch because the cooler weather will allow a lawn to recover much faster. Removing excess thatch will allow water, sunlight, and oxygen to reach starving and choked root systems.

During the cool damp weather of spring, certain diseases such as leaf spot will appear. Fungicides will keep these diseases in check. When the hot weather arrives, many of these diseases will melt away.

MAY

There is still time (especially in the cooler north of this zone) to plant grass. For any warm season grasses that might need to be planted, this is about the best time of all.

If a lot of rain is falling and washing nutrients from the lighter soils, it is a good idea to place down an extra application of fertilizer. If weekly programs are being incorporated, be sure to follow the schedule regularly.

If a lawn has not yet been power raked, it is still time to have this job done and get the full benefit of the process.

Aerating for spring wakeup is still a good idea if it has not been done already.

If preemergence controls for weeds were not used earlier, the weeds will now begin to show. Dandelions and crabgrass are the easiest to see. If the weather has not yet reached a steady 85 degrees Fahrenheit this is the best time to use postemergence herbicides.

JUNE

Continue scheduled fertilizing. Cool season grasses store up nutrients that are applied at this time to use during the heat of summer.

Watering programs in all southern states and most northern states should be fully implemented by the middle of June. Deep watering should be utilized. As the daytime temperatures reach over 90 degrees Fahrenheit, brown patches of dry grass will begin to show and should be expected wherever insufficient moisture reaches the roots.

As the heat increases, most weeds are best removed by hand or by weekly mowing, since most chemicals will not work well in temperatures over 85 degrees. Certain annual grasses will begin to grow and then will turn brown and die in the heat of summer. These can be dealt with by applied chemicals in most of the northern or high-elevation areas where the weather is still cool enough. In other states it's best to wait until fall.

Cutworms will begin to appear in June. These worms love hot weather and your grass will suffer accordingly. If you have had cutworms before, it is good to treat a lawn for them now. They are evidenced by brown and dying grass that will pull free with no attachment to any roots. Sod webworms will also become evident. The moths can be seen flying low over lawns and the worms themselves can be observed at night as they feed. Cutting and lifting up a square of sod can bring both pests to light. Use appropriate chemical controls or they can spread very quickly, especially in the cooler Rocky Mountain areas.

JULY TO AUGUST

In this hot weather, many cool season grasses will become almost dormant. Good watering and good fertilizing will help keep these lawns green. Most yellow and brown spots are the result of heat and insufficient moisture. Keep watering on an appropriate schedule.

Even if aeration has been done in the spring, many of the holes will be closed up and filled in by this time and another aeration job should be performed for maximum summer water use and greening.

Grubs will be plentiful during these two months. They will eat the roots of your lawn and the blades will pull free with no trouble. There are many different treatments for grubs. Many of these treatments can be used during even these hot summer months. Read labels for correct application. One point to remember is that no matter what chemical is applied, it is best to water thoroughly to help chemicals filter down more easily into the lawn.

SEPTEMBER

As the hot days decrease and the warm days with cool nights take over, the best planting season of the year arrives. Cool season grasses will become established in plenty of time to survive the harsh winter months.

Fertilizer that is applied during this month will strengthen and restore lawns that have been depleted by the summer heat. Fertilizer schedules should be followed closely.

Power raking can be performed with excellent results during these cooler days if it is needed. This will provide better use of fertilizer and sun for the remaining growing season.

Preemergence chemicals can be applied in later September to rid lawns of annual grasses that will seed next spring. Postemergence controls can also be safely used for persistent broad-leaved weeds.

The last few weeks of September and the first few weeks of October are another excellent time to aerate, even if this procedure has been done already during the spring and summer. This will help fight molds, spore growth, and diseases that appear from fall and winter rains.

OCTOBER

Good planting weather for cool season grasses will continue for several weeks in the southern areas that are warm.

As broad-leaved weeds continue to grow, it is still good enough weather for most of the month to use postemergence controls.

This is a good time to overseed and add new mixtures of grass that might have strengths that your present lawn might lack.

In the higher altitudes it is time to use fungicides for snow mold if it was a problem last year. The disease organisms will still be present and awaiting the right conditions to appear. Before any chemicals are used it is wise to check all labels and closely follow directions for use.

One last fertilizer application should be laid down. This fertilizer will be stored by the grass for use during the harsh winter months.

The last lawn mowing of the year should be short to keep the long blades of grass from compacting and fostering a place for disease. This will help in spring cleanup next year.

16 ❧ Troubleshooting

TROUBLE
BUMPY AND UNEVEN LAWN SURFACE

POSSIBLE CAUSES
- Worms coming to the surface.
- Tree roots growing near the surface.
- Presence of gophers and/or field gophers.

POSSIBLE REMEDIES
1. Worms rise to the surface and create mounds in an attempt to get oxygen into the soil. To alleviate this problem it is wise to aerate.
2. To keep soils from compacting and locking out oxygen, use a drop spreader or broadcast spreader to lay down a layer of sand (never more that a quarter inch per application) over a lawn area to improve drainage. If a lawn is aerated first, the sand will trickle down in and fill up the holes for better distribution. This procedure may need to be

repeated several times over a three year period to create the best drainage effect.

3. It is possible to use specific chemicals to get rid of worms. This is not always recommended because night crawlers are usually more beneficial than damaging.

4. Tree roots grow near a surface when water is only available on the surface for them to use. Watering programs set for long periods will encourage roots to seek farther down for water.

5. Remove all grass and cut out all problem roots. Then the grass can be replanted in clear soil. This is difficult and expensive but is sometimes necessary. Water for long periods after this renovation is done so that the problem does not arise again.

6. Gophers and their smaller cousins the field gophers love the soft soil of lawns. It is usually necessary to trap or poison these pests. Their holes must then be filled in well before a lawn surface will be even and able to support grass over the entire area.

TROUBLE
MOSS GROWING ON THE SURFACE OF THE SOIL

POSSIBLE CAUSES
- Too much shade covering this section of lawn.
- Poor water drainage.
- Improper fertilization.

POSSIBLE REMEDIES
1. If trees are causing shaded areas that block out the sun for most of the day, clear away all low branches and any dead branches. This will allow some light into a sunlight-starved lawn. As the lawn strengthens, it will fight off most mosses.

2. Aerate to allow proper drainage. As the surface water is drained off, the moss will not have enough moisture to survive on.

3. Use ammonium sulfate to burn out moss. This will work quite well, but unless the problem that caused the moss to appear in the first place is remedied, it will return.

4. Plant a grass that is strengthened to grow in shade. A strong grass will not allow moss to grow.

TROUBLE
A LAWN GROWING THIN AND SPARSE

POSSIBLE CAUSES
- Poor fertilization.
- Poor soil content.
- Compacted soil.
- Improper watering procedures.
- Presence of grass diseases.

POSSIBLE REMEDIES
1. If the problem is fertilization, begin to follow a regular fertilizing program. Be certain that iron and nitrogen are components of any fertilizer used.
2. If the soil content has too much clay, it is possible to aerate a lawn and then spread a light layer of sand that will fill in the holes, mix with the clay, and begin to help drainage. But if loam or clay need to be added, it might be necessary to start over with a new lawn after first laying down a good base of soil. This is a drastic measure but is in some circumstances quite necessary.
3. If a lawn is thin because water is not provided in appropriate amounts, a new watering procedure must be implemented. This new procedure should consist of a regular schedule and more uniform coverage.
4. If after studying symptoms closely a disease seems possible, retain a professional to check for lawn diseases. If any diseases are found and confirmed, chemical procedures may be called for. Check with the professional before implementing.

TROUBLE
GRASS GROWING THIN IN AREAS SHADED BY TREES OR BUILDINGS

POSSIBLE CAUSES
- If grass is growing thin under trees it can be because tree roots are pulling all available water from the soil.
- The wrong variety of grass could be planted in the area.
- It is possible that not enough sunlight is present for any variety of grass to grow.

POSSIBLE REMEDIES

1. If tree roots are pulling the water from the soil, it is necessary to increase the amount of watering time under trees so that water will penetrate the soil to a depth of three feet or more. This will encourage trees to seek deeper for water and to leave the surface alone. This should also leave enough water for both the tree and the lawn to flourish.
2. If the problem is that the wrong variety of grass has been planted in the shade of a building or tree, it will help to aerate the thin area and then overseed with a specific shade grass.
3. If the sunlight is too sparse to grow any type of grass under a tree, try cutting back branches that are low to the ground or dead. Cut back as many as possible to allow sunlight to penetrate.
4. If the building or tree is not allowing enough sunlight for any grass to grow, try cutting away what grass is left and putting in a border garden or flower bed that utilizes shade flowers or plants.

TROUBLE
GREAT AMOUNTS OF WEEDS GROWING

POSSIBLE CAUSES
- A field or uncultured plot of ground close by that is allowing many hundreds of times the average amount of weed seeds to continuously replant themselves.
- The lawn is being cut too short, allowing weed seeds to take an easy hold in the weakened grass.
- Poor watering procedures that create a weakened lawn where weeds easily take root.
- Poor fertilizing procedures that create a weakened lawn where weeds easily take root.
- Wrong variety of grass planted in the area that only grows weakly and allows weeds to take hold.

POSSIBLE REMEDIES

1. If a field close by spreads a great amount of weeds into your lawn, it is best to use copious amounts of preemergence and postemergence chemical controls. If some good herbicides are used on a regular basis, a soil will remain as weed-free as is possible under such circumstances.
2. If a lawn is being cut almost to the crown, allow the grass to grow longer before cutting. This will serve to strengthen a lawn and thus keep weeds

from growing well. This will also save a great deal on water loss due to evaporation.

3. A lawn that has hard-packed soil with no sign of water penetration usually suffers from incorrect watering. Aerate the soil well and institute a program of long periods of watering for deep penetration. This will strengthen the grass and allow it to fight back against weeds.

4. A lawn that is a constant yellow with thin blades is usually deficient of fertilizer. If this is the case, utilize correct fertilizing procedures to strengthen a lawn against weed incursion.

5. If no time is available for ascertaining the causes, retain a professional to figure out the problem and suggest the right chemical or necessary procedure.

TROUBLE
GRASS GROWING IN CLUMPS

POSSIBLE CAUSES
- Presence of crabgrass growing in the lawn.
- Poor soil content.
- Presence of toxic chemicals in the soil.
- Wrong variety of grass mixture.

POSSIBLE REMEDIES
1. If crabgrass is present, it will be necessary to either dig the offending clumps out, use postemergence chemicals to kill the grasses, or wait until spring or fall to spray preemergence chemicals.

2. If the soil is nutrient-poor, it will need to be enriched with mulch, loam, and fertilizer in generous quantities. This can be done without removing the already present lawn as long as the new nutrients are spread minimally thinly and evenly over the entire lawn.

3. If the lawn grows in clumps of thick and healthy lawn and clumps of thin and sick lawn it can be because chemicals that weaken grass are present in the lawn. The first answer to this problem is to spread a layer of nutrient soil over the whole lawn, wait until the grass grows up over this new soil, and then place down another layer. Repeat this procedure until several inches of nutrient-rich soil cover the bad soil and the lawn is able to grow better. The second option is to totally remove all of the grass and lawn to a depth of 6 inches or more. Then fill in the space with grade A soil and replant the lawn with either sod, seed, or sprigs.

4. If the grass grows in clumps because of the presence of a fine grass

mixed in with a coarse grass, the only options are to either overseed the entire lawn with the coarse strain or to remove the entire lawn and replant with the right blend of grass variety.

TROUBLE

PUDDLES OF WATER FORMING THROUGHOUT PORTIONS OF THE LAWN SURFACE

POSSIBLE CAUSES
- Clay soil creating poor drainage.
- Soil compaction.
- Uneven lawn surface.

POSSIBLE REMEDIES
1. A clay soil is present in a problematical quantity many difficulties will arise. The worst problem is that of the clay baking into rocklike consistency when the heat of summer arrives. When clay soil bakes like this, grass roots cannot survive for any length of time. To alleviate this problem you must aerate extensively and then spread sand over the lawn in an even layer that will fill in the aeration holes and thus change the clay composition to a lighter and more drainable mixture.
2. Soil compaction is what happens when there is a lot of traffic on a lawn and the soil is pressed tightly down to the point where plant roots cannot breathe or get moisture through the tight pressure surrounding them. Compaction will also occur when water in heavy torrents from frequent rains falls on a lawn, or just when sprinklers are used that spray water high and far to drop heavily on a lawn. Compaction will also happen when animals such as dogs make frequent use of a lawn, running and moving around on it.

   When compaction is a problem, the remedy is exactly the same as for clay. You must aerate at least three times a year and, whenever possible, spread in soils such as sand that will be lighter in composition. It can also be wise to change the conditions that are causing the compaction— perhaps restrict the traffic or change to a different sprinkler type. These changes are options that are not always easy or possible.
3. Sometimes a lawn will have shallow depressions in the surface makeup; perhaps it was not rolled before the grass was planted or perhaps a deep below-the-surface problem has caused the ground to sink. Water will

drain from the higher areas of the lawn and fill these depressions. Grass will have difficulty growing here and soil compaction will occur. These soil depressions should be filled with many thin layers of grade A soil, with several weeks in between each layering to allow the grass to grow up over the new soil. This should continue until the surface is even throughout.

TROUBLE
A LAWN ROOT SYSTEM THAT ONLY GROWS TO A SHALLOW DEPTH

POSSIBLE CAUSES
- Light watering instead of heavy.
- Nutrient-poor soil.
- Hard, compacted soil.

POSSIBLE REMEDIES
1. Grass roots will reach only a shallow depth if water is applied in small amounts many different times rather than in large amounts a few times. Small amounts of water only sink to shallow depths, and when water is to be found in a shallow depth, grass roots will stay there to take advantage of where the moisture is. Shallow root systems, however, dry up faster and burn up more easily in the hot summer sun.

   Water for long periods. This will cause the moisture needed by your lawn to be found in the depths, and with roots growing deeper, a lawn will stay green and thick even in harsh summer weather.
2. If nutrients are not present in soil, roots and blades both will have little to grow on. To get nutrients, institute a heavier, more regular fertilizer program. Add layers of nutrient-rich soil to the lawn whenever possible.
3. Hard, compacted soil causes a lawn to grub and strain for every tiny millimeter of penetration. The remedy for this is covered in the section of this chapter that deals with puddles of water forming on a lawn surface. Aerate and add lighter soil components.

TROUBLE
ENTIRE LAWN APPEARS YELLOW INSTEAD OF GREEN

POSSIBLE CAUSES
- Not enough nutrients in soil.
- Too much thatch.

• Not enough moisture.

POSSIBLE REMEDIES

1. Lack of a certain nutrient will cause a lawn to be yellow. When the soil makeup of a lawn is light and sandy, nutrients will wash out even with normal watering. In this case it is important to add fertilizer on a regular basis. The two main nutrients that when missing will cause a lawn to be yellow are nitrogen and iron. Use a fertilizer that is heavy in these nutrients.

2. When dead grass in the form of thatch is thick and deep in a lawn, the general appearance is yellow instead of green. Power rake a lawn that has one-half inch or more of thatch. For the first week or so of a rake job the lawn will still be yellow because of the particles of dead grass that have been brought to the surface. Water extra for that week and the color will improve.

3. When a lawn utilizes cool season grasses and the summer heat reaches 94 degrees Fahrenheit and above, the appearance of the grass can take on a yellow hue. This is because cool season grasses such as Kentucky bluegrass will go into a semidormant phase to survive this heat. To avoid this dormant period even in the worst heat it is necessary to supply greater amounts of water and fertilizer to the grass so that it does not need to go dormant to survive.

TROUBLE

DIFFERENT-TEXTURED GRASSES

POSSIBLE CAUSES
• Wrong mixture of permanent planted grass.
• Presence of new varieties of grass that have been brought in by animals, wind, or humans.

POSSIBLE REMEDIES

1. There are only two answers to the wrong blend of planted grass. The homeowner must select the hardiest (and this is also usually the coarsest) variety of grass in the present blend and then overseed the entire lawn with this variety. Or the homeowner can remove the entire lawn and start again with the right blend.

2. When a new variety is brought in by some accidental outside means, it will start to invade only a small area at first and then grow outward. This area will appear either finer than the rest of the lawn or coarser. When the invaded area is small it is easy to dig up the entire area (be

129

sure there is not even one blade of grass left to carry on the strain) of different grass and then replace the spot with sod or seed. Sod is usually a quicker replacement, but the correct variety of grass must be matched or the problem will recur.

TROUBLE
DEAD OR DYING BROWN SPOTS

POSSIBLE CAUSES
- Presence of grass-toxic chemicals.
- Presence of lawn pests.
- Deposits of animal refuse.
- Too much fertilizer.
- Presence of lawn disease.

POSSIBLE REMEDIES
1. Retain professional help to analyze chemicals. If one has been spilled (gas is often spilled on lawns when filling mowing machines), it is necessary to remove the dead grass and the soil up to a depth of 5 inches or more. Then fill with new soil and replant the grass.
2. If pests are in the lawn, it is possible to pull up the grass in a brown spot and have it come out easily with no roots attached. Sometimes the dead sod will roll back like a carpet. In this case it is necessary to ascertain the specific pest and to use a suitable chemical means to get rid of it.
3. If animal waste has been left on a lawn for even a short time before being removed it will overload the lawn with fertilizer nutrients. Brown spots will occur. To prevent the brown spots and to help heal those that have already appeared, wash down the spot where the waste has been several different times with ten to fifteen minutes of medium-pressure water. Patiently wait for the grass to grow back. It usually will begin to grow back in three weeks.
4. When too much fertilizer has been laid down in some spot on a lawn, dead brown patches will occur. These spots must be washed down with moderate pressure for half an hour at a time for several days. The grass will return in anywhere from one month to one year, depending on the diligence of the flushing procedure and the amount of fertilizer spilled. Replanting can be done if desired. Soil replacement is not necessary for replanting as long as the area has been flushed several times.
5. If a disease is suspected, it is best to consult a professional. If a disease

is confirmed, ask the same professional for advice on methods of cure. Many cures are listed in this book but a qualified nursery person will be versed in the latest advances in disease control. Follow this advice closely and if possible get a second opinion.

Index

CAMBRIDGESHIRE COLLEGE OF
AGRICULTURE & HORTICULTURE
LIBRARY
LANDBEACH ROAD, MILTON
CAMBRIDGE CB4 4DB